The
Louisville
Review

Volume 89
Spring 2021

THE LOUISVILLE REVIEW

Editor	Sena Jeter Naslund
Associate Editor	Flora K. Schildknecht
Managing Editor	Amy Foos Kapoor
Guest Poetry Editors	Wanda Fries, Maureeen Morehead, Alan J. Naslund
Guest Fiction Editors	Amy Foos Kapoor, Crystal Wilkinson
Cornerstone Editor	Betsy Woods
Intern	Jared M. Foos

TLR publishes two volumes each year: spring and fall. Visit our website for complete guidelines, back issues, subscriptions, and more: www.louisvillereview.org.

Like us on Facebook for up to date information about each issue, news on contributors, etc.: www.facebook.com/TheLouisvilleReview. Follow us on Twitter @TheLouRev.

Questions? Please note our email and mailing addresses:

managingeditor@louisvillereview.org

The Louisville Review Corp.
1436 St. James Court #1
Louisville, Kentucky 40208
www.louisvillereview.org

This issue: $10 ppd
Sample copy: $5 ppd
Subscriptions: One year, $18; two years, $36; three years, $40
Foreign subscribers, please add $35/year for shipping.

The text and the cover printed in the United States. Cover design by Jonathan Weinert. Typesetting of Tibetan script by Ron Schildknecht.

Front cover artwork, Martha Corazon, *Mountain Village*, oil on canvas and paper, 28 x 30 in. Photo by James Norton, N3creative.net.

Back cover artwork, Laurie Fader, *Perseverance*, 2021, oil on canvas, 64 x 54 in. Photo by Ron Schildknecht.

The Louisville Review is a member of the Community of Literary Magazines and Presses.

PROUD MEMBER

In the beginning, I must express thanks to the many individuals and foundations who have so generously made donations that contribute significantly to our ability to publish *The Louisville Review.*

This issue of *TLR* is proud to point out that two Kentucky Poet Laureates accepted our invitation to serve as editors for this issue: newly appointed fiction writer and poet Crystal Wilkinson has participated in selecting fiction in this issue, and Maureen Morehead, a former Kentucky Poet Laureate, 2011-12, also participated in selecting poetry. Two feathers in our cap to have these remarkable women aboard! Come to think of it, fiction-writer-me also served as a Kentucky Poet Laureate in 2005-6, so I guess that's 2 + 1 = 3 happy women who truly love the literary arts.

After nearly two decades of institutional support by the University of Louisville, followed by two decades of support by Spalding University, the newly independent *Louisville Review* is reaching out in new directions, while continuing its invitation to both new and established poets and fiction writers to submit their work to us: translations are welcome if permission has been given. (Please see our website for the dates for open submissions.) Having always believed in the interrelatedness of the arts, we at *TLR* want to begin to feature work by contemporary artists, accompanied by a variety of introductory essays.

On the front cover of this issue, we feature a painted collage by Martha Corazon, née Harrison, titled *Mountain Village,* a low relief sculpture made of hand-torn, painted paper. When I purchased it, some years ago in Boston, from the artist, I especially loved its flamboyant, colorful, non-realistic response both to landscape and to the human creation nestled at its center. It seems a most hopeful and jubilant idea: that we can coexist—mere people and mighty mountains; perhaps people can adapt to nature. The painting is accompanied by a memoir (see p. 13) of its creator, written by her friend, fiction writer Robin Lippincott, who also has written a book about the life and work of modernist painter Joan Mitchell titled *Blue Territory.*

Unlike *Mountain Village* which suggests that the natural world and the village may be seen as part of a harmonious whole, nature perhaps being a guide or providing a pattern for how humankind might structure its assemblage, in Louisville-based artist Laurie Fader's painting *Perseverance*, the human figure, a woman traveler is challenged by the rising water and flotsam of a flooded city. In Biblical lore, the man-made world was destroyed for its wickedness by water; here, perhaps in tandem with scientists' little-heeded global warnings of rising ocean waters, a city is being swamped. In this chaotic world, the female figure that dominates the painting knows her own direction and energy, and the Devil can take the hindmost. *TLR* Associate Editor Flora K. Schildknecht comments on this work in a short essay on p. 15.

Another new direction for the new, independent *TLR* is to embrace the globe more purposefully by including both poetry and fiction by far-flung writers. In this issue, we feature something of the landscape and spirituality of Tibet, by poet Emily Jane O'Dell with co-translations by Sonam Dungtso featuring Tibetan and English script, as well as stories set in Pakistan and Russia, by Samina Hadi-Tabassum and Anastasia Dreval.

In addition to engaging global narratives, this issue of the magazine also connects former times with the current national reckoning with racial injustice. Long ago, there was a city police commissioner in Birmingham, Alabama (where I grew up) who was the epitome of racism and injustice. Now U.S. poet Elizabeth Hughey has a new collection coming out titled *White Bull*, which engages that difficult time, both in its racism and its sexism in repressing girls of any color with antiquated mores. Every poem of Police Commissioner Bull Connor is made from his own words, disassembled and rearranged. We are honored to be able to offer our readers a preview of this amazing collection, to be published in January 2022 by Louisville's stellar press, Sarabande Books, edited by Sarah Gorham.

We'd love to hear from our readers, especially about works you've found particularly interesting for any reason. Please email us at managingeditor@louisvillereview.org or contact us on our Facebook page.

As Editor, I'd like to list and thank the guest editors for this issue of *The Louisville Review*, with much appreciation for your work:

WANDA FRIES received an MFA from Bennington College. Her poetry and fiction have appeared in various journals, most notably *Special Report: Fiction, the Michigan Quarterly Review,* and *New Southerner.* Her poem "Annunciation" received the first prize in the inaugural James Baker Hall Poetry Award. A Bread Loaf Scholar, she has twice received an Al Smith Fellowship from the Kentucky Arts Council. She has taught for 32 years at Somerset Community College and has published two novels, *Ash Grove* and *In the Absence of Angels*, a collection of short stories, *The Vineyard and Other Stories*, and a collection of poetry, *Cassandra Among the Greeks.* She is currently working on a novel about Catherine Blake, wife of the Romantic poet and artist, William Blake.

AMY FOOS KAPOOR is the managing editor of *The Louisville Review,* writer, television/digital media producer, and event coordinator for the annual summer reading series, "Voice & Vision: Presented by Spalding's School of Writing, *The Louisville Review* & 21c Museum Hotel" in Louisville, Kentucky. Her forthcoming picture book, *Into the Blue: A Counting Adventure*, will be published in the fall of 2021 (BeaLu Books). She earned an MFA from Spalding University's School of Creative and Professional Writing, where she studied writing for children and young adults.

MAUREEN MOREHEAD is a poet and a teacher retired from Jefferson County Public Schools and Spalding University's School of Creative and Professional Writing. She has published poems in many literary journals and magazines, including *The American Poetry Review, the Greensboro Review, the Iowa Review,* and *Poetry Magazine.* She's also been published in and served as poetry editor, on occasion, for *The Louisville Review* since its first issue. Morehead has published six collections of poems, four from Larkspur Press, the latest, *The Red Gate.* She served as Kentucky's Poet Laureate from 2011 to 2012.

ALAN J. NASLUND began writing poetry in creative writing classes at the University of Montana and continued as he earned a doctorate at the University of Louisville in 1982. Writing awards he has won include a Kentucky Arts Council Al Smith Fellowship in Fiction, a Sewanee Writers Conference Tennessee Williams Fellowship in Playwriting, a Vermont Studio Center Fellowship in fiction, a national award in poetry from *The Louisville Review,* and an award in playwriting from the

University of Montana. His books are: *Silk Weather* (Fleur de Lis Press), and a novel, *Hob's Way*, an ebook available on Amazon.

Crystal Wilkinson, Kentucky's Poet Laureate, is the award-winning author of *The Birds of Opulence* (winner of the 2016 Ernest J. Gaines Prize for Literary Excellence), *Water Street,* and *Blackberries, Blackberries.* She is the recipient of a 2021 O. Henry Prize and a 2020 USA Artist Fellowship. Nominated for the John Dos Passos Award, the Orange Prize and the Hurston/Wright Legacy Award, she has received recognition from the Yaddo Foundation, Hedgebrook, The Vermont Studio Center for the Arts, The Fine Arts Work Center in Provincetown and others. Her short stories, poems and essays have appeared in numerous journals and anthologies including most recently in *The Kenyon Review, STORY, Agni Literary Journal, Emergence, Oxford American* and *Southern Cultures.* Her fourth book *Perfect Black* is forthcoming from University Press of Kentucky in August 2021. She currently teaches at the University of Kentucky where she is Associate Professor of English in the MFA in Creative Writing Program.

Betsy Woods is an author, editor, and teacher. Her work has appeared in *The Louisville Review, The New Orleans Review, The Trunk, Alive Now, Literally Stories, The Times-Picayune, ACRES USA, Sophisticated Woman, Citizens Together, The Burningword Literary Journal,* the *Children's Literature Association*, and others. She is the editor of Cornerstone of *The Louisville Review*, past writer and researcher for The Louis Armstrong House Museum, and writer-in-residence at The Waldorf School of New Orleans. She has an MFA in writing from Spalding University. New Orleans is her home; she grew up on the shores of Lake Pontchartrain and on the edge of Doubloon Bayou where she listened to alligators bark. She shares a rooted heritage with the wetlands. They intermingle in her, like lily pad roots.

–Sena Jeter Naslund, Editor

FICTION

BOOK REVIEWS

CORNERSTONE
work by writers K-12

Robin Lippincott

A Door Swung Open: In Memory of Martha Harrison

A native of Enon, Ohio, she had the Midwest written all over, from her wheat-blonde hair to her wide, open face; she looked like the proverbial girl next door but was far more interesting than that All-American construct.

We met 37 years ago working together in a bookstore in Cambridge, Massachusetts. She was an old soul in the body of a beautiful young woman; once I saw her artwork, I was equally dazzled by her talent. She had the best eye of anyone I'd ever known. We became fast friends.

She was an artist who relished words; I was—and am—a writer who loves art. And so, we bandied them about, words, sometimes at rapid-fire pace, one-upping each other with the latest addition to our vocabulary, each trying to outdo the other, bantering, calling forth synonyms, enticed and energized: it was fun!

She was fearless and sure in her art in a way that she never was in her life. She knew she was good, and yet she had no ambition, was not at all career-minded. She married (and later divorced) Rodrigo Correa; together, they fused their names to make Corazon, "heart" in Spanish. And they also made a son, Ezra, who—in his chubby infancy—we called Ezra Poundcake.

Many years into our friendship, I sat down with M. to help her craft something of an artist's statement. She recalled sitting (as a child) at a long, rectangular table, drawing and coloring with five of her eight siblings; it was to distract them from the toys they didn't have, she said. Under the influence of her oldest brother, she enjoyed portraiture and fashion design. But once she was on her own in Chicago, before long, the human face, figure, or any form of realism or representation no longer interested her. One day, she took all of her charcoal portraits out to the dumpster behind her apartment building. "It seemed to me that there was a hierarchy of what was worth looking at," she said, "and the abstract expressionists, whose work I saw at the Art Institute, were expanding and exploding what it was: I realized I wanted to be a part of that." While she would continue to appreciate representational work, she was no longer interested in making it.

Though largely self-taught, she took classes wherever she lived, which included studying with Chicago sculptor Elliot Balter, as well as at Boston's School of the Museum of Fine Arts.

"I love the silence of painting and looking at painting," she said, citing this quote from the writer Deborah Eisenberg as accurately portraying her feelings about both: "Looking at a painting takes a certain composure, a certain resolve, but when you really do look at one it can be like a door swinging open, a sensation, however brief, of vaulting freedom. It's as if, for a moment, you were a different person, with different eyes and different capacities and a different history—a sensation, really, that's a lot like hope."

Friendships open doors (and eyes), too.

Like Joan Mitchell, whose work she admired, M. was a master colorist; she also had a phenomenal sense of composition. Her paintings and collages were often sculptural, and almost always textural; she frequently incorporated various found objects, and other natural elements, into her work: chair caning, beach sand, flowers, leaves, sticks, torn canvas, cloth, cardboard, wood, metal. . . .

We looked at so much art together over the years—hers, that of other artist-friends, in galleries and museums in the Boston area, in New York City, in fact, all over the Northeast; there were many road trips, most with my late partner, Lee, and often with Ezra, too, for the express purpose of seeing this exhibit or that museum. We continually opened each other's eyes and ears.

I have so many of M.'s paintings and collages, most of which she made for me, a few of which I bought. In those works, and through those works, I will always see her, and feel seen by her. And in that way, we will continue to communicate for as long as I'm alive.

Flora K. Schildknecht

Re/visioning Female Resistance: *Perseverance* by Laurie Fader

In Laurie Fader's *Perseverance*, a nude female figure strides across a field of geometric and organic forms. The environment seems to be in a state of collapse—buildings, half submerged by floodwaters, tumble overtop of one another on a canvas electrified with color. The woman swings her elastic, stick-thin arms, her legs seem to have multiplied with the force of her stride, a cloud of small points of light radiate upward from her head, her dark hair, pulled into two tight buns, references the cartoon character Olive Oyl. She is powerful, she is in motion, and she is also unapologetically old.

Perseverance confronts viewers with the aged female body. The bowed back, the heavy thigh, the deflated breasts of the figure tell of a story of a body that has lived—and a body that perseveres: the figure moves forward undeterred, a slight smile on her face, through a world in chaos. Gesturing toward a revision of the notion that only young or unmarked female bodies are capable or worthy, Fader has cast the heroic figure of *Perseverance* as an old woman.

Speaking about *Perseverance*, Fader says that she adapted the painting from an earlier work from her *Vestal Virgin* series. Inspired by the ancient Roman Vestals, women who had the esteemed position of guarding the eternal flame—but who were ruthlessly punished if they broke their vows of chastity—the series focused on stylized female figures who raced through threatening environments, "trying to rescue whatever was there or trying to survive whatever was happening." In the revision of the original, the woman in *Perseverance* has transformed from an abstracted form to a female body which insists that viewers acknowledge its human physicality; viewers encounter both the strength and vulnerability of the woman as she moves through the disintegrating environment. Female resistance to destructive forces is on full display here.

And yet, despite the high stakes implied by this narrative of resisting catastrophe, *Perseverance* is infused with a subversive sense of joy. Through the use of a riotous color palate and abstracted, absurdist organic forms—such as the giant rose-and-yellow foot which dominates the foreground of the painting—*Perseverance* engages the unexpected pleasures of color and of an imagined landscape. This bold use of color and of physical humor can be read as kind of resistance in itself. One senses that the heroic woman in the painting does not merely survive; she continues onward with a determined sense of joy and with a willingness to embrace the absurd. In the current moment—one in which environmental degradation, misogyny, racism, as well as a global pandemic, often seem to threaten at every turn—perhaps such a re-envisioning of female strength is exactly what is called for.

Elizabeth Hughey

THE PAPERS OF BULL CONNOR

Snow falls in the form of a last name
in your letters. It is always snowing
in Alabama in black and white
from your typewriter that sits
on the desk of 1962 with ring marks
and ash. I'll take the words you left
for us and make new colors to wear
on my lips, in *Oxblood*, in *Trampled
Plum*, I will try to kiss the history
out of your words, kiss a cut rose
out of the prosecutor, a summer peach
from the winter impeachment.
I will use only your words, now.
I'll try not to be afraid to kiss
the cottonmouth on the mouth
and the filthy mule, the hot iron.
When I ask your words
what they did, they'll say nothing.
They can't remember
how they were used. They can be
grooms for everyone to marry, again.
They can be teardrop gemstones,
palm leaves, skyrockets. The little
black periods in your letters may grow,
now, to be whole notes, whole nights
released from their blindfolds.

Elizabeth Hughey

THE BELONGINGS

We have to work
with what has been
handed down to us.
We eat off of the words
our grandfathers said.
We sleep in them.
We set our drinks
down upon them.

What were we to do
with the fur stoles
but wear them
to museum balls
on the mildest
of winter nights
heat heavy
on our shoulders
like a burn from the sun
in our great-great-
grandmother's vacation.

We see our reflections
in the sterling set
that we have cleaned
of its meaning.
We could not blame
the knife
for what it divided.
We could not blame
stairs for our falls
or blame the art
for what was praised.

We could not destroy
every thing that was touched.

We still have billfolds,
swimming pools, hangovers,
wingbacks. We had to keep
birdfeeders, cake plates,
neckties and dice.
We kept all of the letters.
We kept all of the trees.

We moved into the names
that were left for us,
and we changed
the locks. Inside
we feel different now,
all sunwink, all meteorite,
but our windows
still look out
over the same city
of unearned suffering
we will not save.

Elizabeth Hughey

A Finger Holds Down a Key

When there's fog in this city
streetlights at dawn up on the hill
get to be campfires at sundown
like the ones in books about war
where the soldiers settle in
for the night while a day's ride
away, ladies are being laced
into their party dresses,
but the party will only be
so much fun, knowing that soldiers
are blowing into their hands
feeling their deaths as close
as dance partners.
Then, the morning light pulls
the fog away like a boy
carrying his bedcovers
and the fires put themselves out
and a red bird scars the air.

Elizabeth Hughey

Forever Bull

I'm always afraid to come back to you
and stand at the fence of your white
pasture, white heat, white grass, white
flies. The only black is in the middle
of your one good eye. White Bull.

By now, I know what I can take
from you. I love your words torn apart
and tied up like colored flags.

From your white mud, you gave me wishbones,
black holes, hairpins, wave pools.
I stand by the waterfall we make together.
I'm going to say, I love you, now, because
you left the words to say it.
I love you, now.

I write you back into your pen
where you will always be. A flag
lets out a prayer over your white body,
   when the wind.

Emily Jane O'Dell

Breath in Tibet

བོད་ཡུལ་དུ་དབུགས་ལེན་པ།

I can't breathe in Tibet.

ངས་བོད་ཡུལ་དུ་དབུགས་ལེན་ཐུབ་ཀྱི་མི་འདུག།

In Tagong–
the place the Bodhisattva likes–
I was reborn
at 13,500 feet.

དཔལ་སྤ་སྒང་།
འཐབས་པའི་སྤ་དགའ་བའི་གནས་མཆོག།
མཚོ་ངོས་ལས་ཨེན་ཁྲུ་༡༣༥༠༠ཡོད་པའི་གནས་འདིར།
ངས་སྐྱེ་བ་ཡང་བསྐྱར་བླངས།

The valley hidden
beneath my tongue
swelled
so high
it pushed my tongue
to the roof of my mouth
until
I could not speak.

ཁྲས་པའི་ལྗང་ཆུང་འདིར།
ངའི་ལྗེ་ཆུང་གི་འོག་དུ།
སྦངས་ཕོག་ནས།
རིམ་གྱིས་འབུར།
ངས་སྐད་ཆ་བཀད་མི་ཐུབ་པའི་བར་དུ།
ལྗེ་ཆུང་ནི་ཡ་མཁལ་གྱི་ཀན་ལ་བཏེགས།

The slopes of this summit
turned
so white
they silenced my cries
to the distant crown
of
the Second Shambhala.

གཡང་གཟར་བའི་རི་སྐྱང་ནས།
རྒྱུབ་ཏུ་འཁོར་ན།
ཅི་འདྲའི་དཀར་སྣང་སྣང་ཞིག།
ཐམ་བླ་ལ་གཉིས་པའི་མཆན་དུ་གསོལ་བའི་རྒྱུང་རིང་གི་ཕྲོག་ཤུ་འདི་ཡིས།
ངའི་སྐྱེ་ངག་ཐམས་ཅད་དྲག་ཏུ་མནན།

The nodes in my neck
grew
as big
as snow lotus bulbs
that squeezed
the stalk
of my throat
until
I could not
breathe.

ངའི་སྐེ་ཡི་སྐྲངས་འབུར་ནི།
རྡེ་ཆེ་ནས་རྡེ་ཆེར་འཕར་ཏེ།
གངས་སྟ་མེ་ཏོག་ལྷ་བྱར་གྱུར།
ངའི་མགྲིན་པར།
དབུགས་ལེན་མི་ཐུབ་པའི་བར་དུ།
རིམ་གྱིས་བཙིར།

Their blossoming will be my death,
I thought.

ངའི་བསམ་པ་ལ།
སྐྱངས་སྒྲུབས་དེ་རལ་དུས་ང་རང་འཆི་འིས་སྣྱམ།

But instead of a blooming,
the water at their roots
erupted from
the riverbed of my
mouth
and gushed forth
like
a Himalayan
spring,
leaving
the gum under my tongue
scraped to the bone–
a polished stone.

ཡིན་འང་། སྐྱངས་སྒྲུབས་ཀྱི་ཁ་ནི་མ་རལ་ཞིང་།
ཚ་བའི་ཆུ་མིར་ནི།
ང་ཡི་ཁ་ནས་ཕྱི་ལ་དྲག་ཏུ་ཕོར།
ཧི་མ་ལ་ཡའི་དཔྱིད་ཀ་ནི་རིམ་གྱིས་ཕྱིན་པ་དང་།
ངའི་སྐྱེ་འོག་གི་ཐང་ཚུ་ནི་རུས་པ་དང་འདྲ་བའི།
རྡྱ་གོར་གོར་ཞིག་གི་སྟེང་ལ་བབས།

The doctors called it a mutant mystery.

The dentist—a tooth infection.

The monks—enlightenment.

སྨན་པ་ཡིས། དེ་ནི་ཐོལ་བྱུང་ཡིན་པའི་ལེ་མཚར་དུ་གཏམ།

སོའི་སྨན་པས། དེ་ནི་སོའི་གཉེན་ཁ་རེད་ཅེས་སྨྲས།

མེར་མོ་བས། ཉམས་རྟོགས་ཀྱི་རྟགས་སུ་བཤད།

Now, I am in exile
in the heart
of Chengdu

ད་སྟུར། ང་རང་ཕྱི་ལ་ཐོན་ནས།
ཐོས་ཐུན་གྲོང་གི་ལྗེ་བར་གནས་ཡོད།

Stopped at
a traffic light
under an overpass.

ཟམ་འོག་རྒྱ་ལམ་ནས།
འགྲིམ་འགྲུལ་སྒྲོག་བཏང་ལ་སྒུག་ནས་ཡོད།

Where a musician
is practicing
scales on
the
saxophone

འདི་གར། རོལ་མོ་བ་ཞིག་གིས།
སྒྲུང་ཁ་ནས།
ལག་སོན་རྫོན་གྱི་སྒྱིང་བུ་སྒྲོང་བཞིན་འདུག

And
we are
choking
on
exhaust
and
jazz.

དེ་བཞིན།
ང་ཚོ་ཡང་།
ངལ་དུབ་དང་ཇ་ཙོ་རོལ་མོ་ཡི་ཅ་ཚོ་འོག་ནས།
དབུགས་ལེན་ཐུབ་ཀྱི་མི་འདུག།

translated to Tibetan by the author and Sonam Dungsto

Emily Jane O'Dell

Meditation Cave

སྒྲུབ་ཕུག།

"Samsara is an ocean of suffering,"
I shout in nomadic dialect
to a Tibetan nun
stepping out of
her cliff cave
to greet me.

འཁོར་བ་ནི་སྡུག་བསྔལ་གྱི་རྒྱ་མཚོའོ།།
ཞེས་ང་ཡིས་འབྲོག་སྐད་ཀྱིས་དེ་ལྟར་བསྒྲགས།
རྡོ་མོ་ཞིག་སྒྲུབ་ཕུག་ནས་ཕྱིན་ལ་བུད་ཀྱང་།
ཁོང་མོའི་སྒྲུབ་ཕུག་གིས།
ང་ལ་འཚམས་བརྗེ་ཞིག་བཏང་སོང་།

"Yes, yes!" she smiles and waves.

ཡིན་དང་ཡིན་ཞེས་འཛུམ་ཞལ་དང་བཅས་ཁོང་
མོས་ང་ལ་ཕྱག་བརྗེ་བཏང་།

How do you say:

ཁྱེད་ཀྱིས་ཅི་ལྟར་གསུངས་པ་ཡིན་ནམ།

In my dreams,
lamas reveal secrets–
teach me how to fly.

ང་ཡི་རྨི་ལམ་དུ།
བླ་བ་རྣམས་ཀྱིས་གསང་བ་བཏོན་ཏེ།
ང་རང་ལ་འཕུར་རྩལ་བསླབས།

On the steep climb
to Ake Tseby's
meditation cave,
every breath counts.

གཟར་བའི་གཡང་ཁ་ནས།
ཨ་ཁུ་ཚེ་སྦྱེ་ཡི་སྒྲུབ་ཕུག་བར་དུ།
དབུགས་ལེན་ཐེངས་རེ་རེ་ལ།

Are these ashes
in my hands
mine or yours?

ང་འི་ལག་ཏུ་ཡོད་པ་རྣམས་ནི།
ང་ཡིའམ་ཁྱེད་ཀྱི་གདུང་ཐལ་ཡིན་ནམ།

Where do you end
and I begin?

ཁྱེད་རང་གང་ནས་འཕོས་པ་ན།
དེར་ང་ཡིས་དབུ་འཛུགས་ཀྱི་ཡིན།

You are being
reborn
while I keep
going
in
circles
around these
prayer wheels.

ཁྱོད་རང་གིས།
སྐྱེ་བ་བསྐྱར་དུ་ལེན་བཞིན་འདུག
ཨ་ཅིའི་འཁོར་ལོ་བསྐོར་ནས།
སྐོར་ལམ་དུ།
གསོལ་བ་ཡང་ཡང་བཏབ།

Om mani padme hum.
Om mani padme hum.
Om mani padme hum.

ཨོཾ་མ་ཎི་པདྨེ་ཧཱུྃ།
ཨོཾ་མ་ཎི་པདྨེ་ཧཱུྃ།
ཨོཾ་མ་ཎི་པདྨེ་ཧཱུྃ།

I want to be reborn
with you.

ངས་ཁྱེད་རང་དང་མཉམ་དུ་ཡང་བསྐྱར་སྐྱེ་བ་ཞིག་ལེན་ན་བསམ་སོང་།

On the altar of
the shrine,
I sprinkle your ashes
when no one is
looking.

སུས་ཀྱང་ལྟ་བཞིན་མེད་པའི་དུས་ན།
ངས་ཁྱེད་ཀྱི་གདུང་ཐལ་དེ།
མཆོད་པའི་རྟེན་གྱི་སྟེང་དུ་བཏབ།

From the mouth of the cave,
I bury you in the sky.

སྤུག་ཕུག་གི་ཁ་ནས།
ངས་ཁྱེད་ཀྱི་སྤུར་ནི་དགུང་སྔོན་དབྱིངས་ལ་བཏབ།

But before you
fall like snow
on the nunnery
below,
the wind carries
you back to me,
and
I inhale
the dust of
of your
blessed bones.

ཁྱེད་རང་ཁ་བ་བཞིན་ལྷུང་ལྷུང་དུ་མར་ལ་བབས་ཤིང་།
དགོན་པའི་མཁའ་དབྱིངས་ནས་ཕྱུར་དུ་ལྡང་།
ལྷག་རླུང་གིས་ཁྱེར་ཏེ། ང་ཡི་འགྲམ་དུ་ལོག
ངས་དབུགས་ལེན་བཞིན།
ཁྱེད་ཀྱི་བྱིན་ཅན་གྱི་གདུང་ཐལ་ལ་ཏྲབ།

You are buried inside me.
ཁྱེད་རང་ངའི་ཤ་ཁྲག་ཚས་གསུམ་དུ་སྦག

Take these vows
every morning
like medicine,
my abbess in
Mongolia
said.

ཉིན་རེའི་ཞོགས་པར།
དམ་ཚིག་འདི་དག་སྨན་བཞིན་དུ་བསྟེན་ཞིག
ཅེས་ངའི་སོག་ཡུལ་གྱི་བླ་མ་ཞིག་གིས་འདི་ལྟར་གསུངས།

Instead, I wake up,
and line my eyes with kohl.

དོན་དུ། ང་རང་སད་དུས།
ངའི་ཨེག་དང་སྐྱོལ་གཉིས་ཕན་ཚུན་ཆེར་རེ་བསྒས་འདུག

Yesterday,
the x-ray
showed the cause
of my chest pain–
prayer beads
tangled around my heart.

ཁ་སང་། X འོད་ཐིག་ལས།
གསལ་བ་ལྟར་ན།
ངའི་སྙིང་ཁ་ན་བ་ནི།
ཕྲེང་བ་ཡིས་ངའི་སྙིང་ཁ་བསྐོར་ཡོད་པ་དང་།

And my cough–
your ashes
clouding my lungs.

ང་སྒོ་རྒྱག་པ་ཡང་།
ཁྱེད་ཀྱི་གདུང་ཐལ་གྱིས་ངའི་གློ་ཁ་འཆུབ་པས་རེད།

Your dust will never leave me.

Your dust is my breath.

I am reborn in you.

ཁྱེད་ཀྱི་གདུང་ཐལ་ནི་ནམ་ཡང་ང་དང་འབྲལ་མི་སྲིད་ལ།

ཁྱེད་ཀྱི་གདུང་ཐལ་ནི་ངའི་དབུགས་ཀྱི་འབྱིན་རྔུབ་ཡིན།

ཁྱེད་ཀྱིས་ཁྱབ་པའི་ལུས་རྟེན་ཞིག་ཏུ་ངས་སྐྱེ་བ་ཡང་བསྐྱར་ལེན་བཞིན་ཡོད།

translated to Tibetan by the author and Sonam Dungsto

Emily Jane O'Dell

TIBETAN CODE

བོད་ཀྱི་གསང་བྱང་།

I mastered nomadic dialect
to meet you.

ངས་འབྲོག་སྐད་བྱང་ཆུབ་པ་ཞིག་སྦྱངས་ནས།
ཁྱེད་རང་དང་མཇལ་ཞིང་།

Climbed 14,000 feet
to reach you.

ཨིན་ཁྱུ༤༠༠༠་ལྡག་ལ་འཛེགས་ནས།
ཁྱེད་རང་སྙེད།

But here, in Tibet,
the price of my kissing you
is death.

ཡིན་འང་། འདིར། བོད་ཡུལ་ན།
ཁྱེད་རང་ལ་ཨོ་ཚམ་བྱེད་པར་ཡང་འཚེ་བའི་རིན་པ་
གཏོང་དགོས།

I don't have the right password to stay.

ང་ལྷའང་འདིར་འདུག་པའི་གསང་བྱངས་ཡང་དག་
དེ་མེད།

You: EPAS-1.

ཁྱེད་རང་། EPAS-1.

Me: COL3A1.

ང་རང་། COL3A1.

On the roof of the world,
your code thrives,
mine dies.

འཛོམ་སྐྱིད་གི་ཡང་རྩེ་འདིར།
ཁྱེད་ཀྱི་གསང་གྲངས་ནི་རིམ་གྱིས་འཕར།
ང་ཡི་གསང་གྲངས་ནི་རིམ་གྱིས་རྒུད།

Mount Yala's winds
whipped the O2
from my blood.
Drowned my lungs
in melting snow.
Froze arteries
into icicles.

བཞག་ཐབ་རི་བོའི་ལྷག་སྐྱང་གི་ཕྱོད་ད།
ང་ཡི་ཁྲག་རྒྱུན་གྱིས་དབུང་དབུགས་ལ་ཡང་ཡང་བསྐུལ།
སྐྱོ་བ་ནི། རིམ་གྱིས་ཞུ་བའི་ཁ་བའི་ནང་དུ་འཐིང་ཞིང་།
འཕར་རྩ་ཡང་། ཆབ་རོམ་གྱི་ཀ་བ་ལྟ་བུར་གྱུར།

But you, like the antelope,
are engineered
to be here.

ཡིན་འང་། ཁྱེད་རང་ནི་རི་དྭགས་གཙོད་དང་འདྲ་བར།
ལས་དབང་གིས་གནས་འདིར་བསྐོས་འདུག།

In 1980, a Tibetan monk
wandered into a holy cave,
and found a jawbone,
instead of enlightenment.

གངས་འབོར།
བྲ་བ་ཞིག སྐྱུབ་ཕུག་འདི་རུ་ཡིབས་པ་དང་།
རྫོགས་པ་མ་གྲོལ་ཞིང་།
ཐོད་རུས་ཤིག་རྙེད།

A gift from your grandpa,
who was 160,000 years old.

ཁྱེད་ཀྱི་ཡབ་མེས་ནས་བརྒྱུད་པའི།
མི་ལོ༡༦༠༠༠༠དང་ལྡན་པའི་ལེགས་སྐྱེས་ཤིག

Your inheritance is from the Denisovans.
Mine is from David,
the father I never met.

ཁྱེད་ཀྱི་ཁག་རྒྱུན་ནི་དེ་ནེ་སོ་ལྷ་དང་།
ང་ཡི་ནི་དྲ་ཝེ་ཞེས་པའི།
ནམ་ཡང་མཇལ་མྱོང་མེད་པའི་ཡབ་ཆེན་དེ་ཡིན།

This variant has not been previously reported.

འགྱུར་རྟོ་འདིའི་གཅས་ལ་སྟོན་དུ་གོ་སྦྱོང་མེད།

DISEASE: Ehlers-Danlos Syndrome, Vascular Type.

ཨེ་ལེར་ཊང་ལོ་སན་ཙོར་ཞེས་པའི་ནད་ཡམས་ཤིག།

My secret code (don't share!):
c.1201G>C:p.A401P (chr2: 189858966 [hg19]).

དའི་གསང་གྲངས་ནེ། གཞན་ལ་མ་བཤད།

c.1201G>C:p.A401P (chr2: 189858966 [hg19]).

*This variant has not been curated
in public variant databases such as ClinVar.*

འགྱུར་རྡོ་འདི་ཞི་ད་དུང་།
བྱི་སྤྱོད་ཀྱི་གྲངས་མཛོད་དུ་འབོད་མེད་པ་ཞིག་རེད།

Never let them curate you, my dear–
stay wild and unknown.

ནམ་ཡང་། གཞན་དབང་གིས་བཀས་སྟོན་བྱེད་དུ་མ་འཇུག་པར།
རྐྱོད་པོ་དང་གསང་བའི་རང་བཞིན་ལ་གནས་པར་གྱུར་ཅིག

On my lifesaving
descent,
a six-story saffron OM
painted in Kangding
guided my sprint
to the ER.

དའི་ཚེ་སྲོག་སྐྱོབ་པའི་དུས།
དར་ཚེ་མདོ་ནས་བྲིས་པའི་ཨོྂ་ཡིག་དམར་པོ་ཞིག་གིས།
ང་རང་གྱུར་སྐྱོབ་ཁང་དུ་ཁྲིད།

OMMMMMMMMMMMMMMMMMM.

ཨོྂ

ཨོྂ

ཨོྂ

Your OM by nature
carries more air.

ཁྱེད་ཀྱི་ཨོྃ་ཡིག་གིས།
མཁའ་དབུགས་མང་ཚམ་ཁྱེར་བྱུང་།

Let me jump in your bloodstream,
so you can carry me up.

ང་རང་ཁྱེད་ཀྱི་ཁྲག་རྒྱུན་དུ་མཆོངས་དུ་བཅུག་ཅིང་།
དེ་ནས་ཁྱེད་ཀྱིས་ང་པང་དུ་སྐྱངས།

This nomad has hit
a boundary
she can't cross.

འབྲོག་པའི་མི་རིགས་འདི་ཆད་ལ་ཕྱག་པའི་སྐབས་འདིར།
ཁོ་མོ་ཡང་ཐར་བ་དཀའ།

This is my final farewell,
my love.

འདི་ནི་ངའི་ཆེས་མཐའ་མཇུག་གི་ཁྱུས་བརྡ་སྟེ།
ང་ཡི་སྙིང་སྡུག་ལགས།

Protect your code—
your natural and
best defense.

ཁྱེད་རང་གི་གསང་གྲངས་ལེགས་པར་སྲུང་དང་།
དེ་ནི་ཁྱེད་ཀྱི་རང་བཞིན་དང་ཆེས་ལེགས་པའི་སྲུང་ཁྱེད་ཡིན།

And look for
the sliver of my
mandible
buried
deep in your snow.

ཁྱེད་ཀྱི་གངས་གཤེབ་དུ་སྦས་པའི།
ངེད་ཀྱི་དངུལ་གྱི་མ་མགལ་དེ་འཚོལ་བཞིན་ཡོད།

translated to Tibetan by the author and Sonam Dungsto

Lily Greenburg

As a Child I Lived in Many Houses, All of Them My Body

Mornings, I slid my hands
through the willow—
like doorframe beads, the branches
parted. I entered the enclosure,
long grass asleep underfoot.

My house now, I thought,
and it was—sticks, I arranged
just so, a hallway, a bedroom.
Robins argued, and I rolled my eyes
like a neighbor. Sun and clouds
turned the lights on and off.

Then, to the sewer—following
crawdads, I blinked in the dark
possibilities (who lived here?).
My flashlight made shadow,

but if I kept going—blue light,
a ladder, the sweep of cars seen
through a drain. I could only look
and turn back, like the end of a dream.

It's morning now. Snow is raining
from my roof gone wet white. I can go
anywhere I want but I don't. Every door
in my house is shut. I sit in my closet
and I am sitting in my closet.

It could be morning forever
and I still wouldn't find myself.
I have a house now, a real one, I say
to the girl I was. She calls back,
Not as real as mine.

Will Simescu

OMENS

> *I have made myself alone now.*
> —W. S. Graham, "Malcolm Mooney's Land"

Ancient pictographs,
minor attractions I view roadside
somewhere near Orangeville, Utah,
mirror an eddy's infinite whorl.
Some symbolize snakes. Others,
as far as anyone can tell,
the wheel of time.

On the Ruth Glacier,
I narrowly avoid a moulin,
a vertical shaft a mile deep or more.
Each spring, rangers find bodies intact
at the glacier terminus, detritus from tunnels
that snake through the ice sheet.

Could I believe in omens,
a goshawk angling
across an aerial Cartesian plane
tearing to pieces two large crows
may convince me once more
to cross the Colorado.

If there is a sublime symmetry,
I hope no one discovers its codices.
Let them rest in silence. Or if not silence,
a wordless creep.

Carl Boon

A Room in Wales

The table symbolized a need,
the need a past she couldn't know,
symbolized by tribulation.

I must know how Father felt
here, where I am, during the War
when it was not won, when the room
smelled of candlesmoke and pears

and the children outside knocked
but couldn't enter. I must know
what I cannot know, she said.

But the past, a brutal thing,
as yet surrounds her, tells her
loneliness is truth and that he left
a week before Christmas Eve,

1917. An afghan remains, a pipe
and a pair of slippers. She stretches
as his world colludes against her.

She stretches toward a glass
of brandy and the grand piano
to winter herself, to drowse for him,
the missing one, the mover.

She grasps at eternity; she feigns
a move toward the slouching cat
then settles, but the past will not.

Marcia L. Hurlow

MOTHER, FRAMED

I sit cross-legged on my bed and watch
Mother hang white sheets along invisible

wires outside. From the basket on the ground
her hands rise with the laundry, her arms stretch

up as in praise. The spring wind blows enough
to puff her pale blue skirt like a bubble.

I know, at seven, I should go out
just to hand her clothespins and wet towels.

Her long brown hair lifts with the breeze
and her feet are hidden, dandelions,
clover and grass up to her ankles.

I recall the bright smell of sun on damp
cloth, and the cheerful lilt of her voice.

Instead I'll wait until she picks up
her empty basket, turns to the house.
For now, her beauty fills my window.

Tara Tulshyan

A Summer Unripening

Where green sab-a peels skip their yellow stage   is where we started.
Now we stand in a pond   of cigarette dust tarnished canvas
      beer bottles opening their mouths to the sun   like the cassavas
that simmer in Guimbal bleached through their open roots.
      We used to sleep on the mud   sumac blanketing our chests
clay curving around our bellies like dough   ready to be baked.
We feed ourselves   with the kangkong roots   swallowing the green
      bark that welts in our throats fermenting our stomachs in an iodine bath.
When jackfruits   burst   the heat begins to fatten   plumping the nipa palm
      whose sap stings the air. This means that it is almost time to leave
gathering the seeds that bury beneath our fingernails   tucking them between rattan
santols split open   flesh thawing blossoming into the terracotta. We add their piths
      to the broth we boil   on the rinds of coconuts   callousing our
tongues when we drink   chewing on peels of plantains if   we couldn't
      fetch rice. When black spots begin to stipple sab-a skins   we must hurry.
Soon, green patches begin to shrivel into the sab-a heads   budworms clambering
      at its flesh   its remains   filling the space where we used to sleep.

Taruni Tangirala

MAYA

Do you remember the scarlet insides of
your Mother's womb
or was it the sun?
I cannot remember.

A Russian doll of dreams vaguely infiltrates
my mind while I try to nap. Am I Russian? No,
Indian, I think
my nose captures the
dulcet pragmatism of cinnamon, sweet Mango

The vedic god Indra teaches us
To smell the lightning and swallow the
Thunder—so that it doesn't burden
mother earth at ground level

In this dream, a peacock spreads sandalwood
upon my eyelids
and I see everything
the spirits of nature encased in emerald auras
the *maya* of the gods
empires of gold, cities
of joy
every truth, every lie consuming their
once-iridescent lives

A hearty bowl of pulav on the table, endlessly
deep like the laughter coming from my bowels
The peacock once again gazes at me—and I can
tell from the profound intuition that its eyes have
gifted me; I still have stories to tell
it's time to go home
it's time to be born.

Lisa Rhoades

If not love

> *people during times of prolonged radical change, end up changing*
> —*New York Times,* April 2020

I was hoping for a softening,
an end to petty cruelties
and a reckoning that's just.
If not ease, at least the shovel
not always hitting stone—
the rocks arranged into a path,
the hold on my heart
loosened just a notch.
So my home becomes a refuge
my marriage a garden, my garden
a bower, lush and not overrun,
because if not peace
then oak, generous and branching,
each year the last to bud,
if not reprieve then the cherry
finishing its bloom, petals
like love letters to the gutters,
the grass. If not love
then sorrow withdrawn, assuaged,
if not blessing then the bumblebee
drunk in the tulip's cup.

Sofia Machado

WHY I HATE WHITE CARPET

when I come home from the hospital
I expect to spend the day cleaning up
the mess I had made
when I couldn't care for myself

instead
I find white carpet

plush under toe
like wood moss
vibrant like the fluorescent
lights in the room
that held me
for so many nights

in my mind's eye
I can see her
gathering the cups of my
depression
dusting away months
of
catatonia

she is not a giver of hugs
does not speak freely with
declarations of love
instead
she
scrapes the sorrow off the windowsill
and tucks joy in with the bedsheets
army style
neat folds
everything in the proper place

there is a swell of something
undefinable
in my chest
and I throw my bag across the room
spilling
clothes
[strings removed]
books
[soft cover only]
and doctor mandated crafts
[to heal]
across the white carpet

the white chasm

the white sea

i have never seen anything
look so much
like
failure

Carl Boon

Uncle Eddie

He turned lathes at U.S. Steel
and phrases into drawn-out stories
in which women—
Scandinavians and Russians,
the occasional Portuguese—
did with their naked bodies
things we could hardly believe.
My mother called him a character,
my grandmother—with her hardened
Slovak stare—scrubbed the chairs
in the kitchen after he departed. I loved him
without knowing why, with whatever love
a boy might muster.

He turned lathes at U.S. Steel
while America slept
and ate ham salad with trembling hands.
Too much booze, they said,
too many whores
pink-skinned, disrobed
along the Allegheny County Line.
But through the madness of America
and his own body failing
in the blue Pennsylvania night,
we agreed he was one of us—
he had to be one of us or else
we weren't. I listened to him as he rocked

on the stoop one Fourth of July, beer
in hand, recounting exploits, burglaries,
Polynesian girls with bright blue lips
who knelt. Who knew the strange
and terrible vastness of America?
Who knew that a man who burped

could know so much?
That they despised him—
sent him where the dog would lie—
revealed something of my country
I must've missed, some facet
of it I should've read about
in study hall, in science class where
the beautiful never was.

David O'Connell

Quarter Acre

The backyard's sandlot dirt till June,
    when violets slip into their seats
among the ant metropolis.

Soon, sensing weakness, the crabgrass
    muscles in, despite my summer
Sunday morning mowing

and the hours on my knees
    prying eyesore dandelion islands up
before they cloud and blow.

By July, the noon sun punching
    triple digits, and little to show
for all my sweat and etiquette,

I shut the sprinklers down,
    peek out behind closed curtains—
a king who's fled his people.

Conditions, predictably, deteriorate.
    Tufts of random weed,
patchy as a teen's first beard,

outpace what grass is left. Nights,
    sweat soaked, I dream the sound
of lawn grubs gnawing roots: a scritch

like tines against the plate. Awake,
    I count the payments down like sheep
till this will all be mine.

Alex Shull

Your name on me

It's a shame your darkest days are behind you
You could have learned more from the pall
Did someone really suffer that way?
Eyes were opened to some horror
Now squinting at a flashlight in pain
Learn from the long whiles who's to blame

What did he think after you looked away?
In your mind, still on that cross, still in agony
You stopped watching before he returned

I will carve out a space for you
In my arms
Is where
Your name belongs
Beneath my armor
Write it here
Across my bony breast
I can read it upside down
Or backwards in a mirror
Or in a photograph

Once I have it down
What will you have to show for it
Other than the scar
Like a magic cigarette hanging from your lip
That never falls or burns

D Larissa Peters

AGE GAP

Was it the whiskey or the cigarettes—or just
years with the earth under the sun?

I'd like to
imagine—as I sit on this curb,
        watching you smoke (so cool and very unlike the boys my
        freshman year in college—nervous and trying not to show it) that
        it was the slow
way you
draw out your
thoughts,
a pull on a hookah and an
exhale of
(to me) (to all those around us)
            profound expression. No mic drop. But a
l o o o n g finish on an
aged scotch.

Please.
Don't disillusion me just yet.

With your age.
With mine.

Kathleen Gregg

Calamata Olives

The salt pricks her taste buds first,
then circulates a slightly bitter, wine-like flavor
over her tongue and palate. Delicious.
She is careful to eat only five of these dark purple
olives, 45 calories.
He keeps count.

She thinks about the burning, relentless
sunshine of Southern Greece; how it invades
the large leaves of this olive variety, arming it
with vitamin A and iron. A healthy indulgence
he allows.

She thinks about their tour of an olive grove;
how she reached out to touch the almond-
shaped fruit; how he grabbed her wrist, jerked
her arm away. He educated her
through clenched teeth. Calamata olives
cannot be harvested green. Once ripe,
they are easily bruised and must be hand-picked.
She could have damaged them.
How would she like that?

She thinks about how they watched the olives
being slit to decrease processing time, then
placed in strong brine to be debittered; how
they were packed in salt, red wine vinegar
and olive oil, the way she loves them; how
he charged past the display of jars for sale,
with a curt shake of his head.

She looks in the mirror, fingers the dark purple
bruise. Her bitterness is ripe, unpalatable.

She thinks about ways her touch could damage
him; how much she would like that.

Peter Cooley

CANTICLE

I've made my compromise with paradise.
Only so much of heaven every day
sings the gold lettering on the morning wind,
only so much allegro before noon,
only so much of evening's pentimento,
only so many angels come to roost
the telephone wire incarnate as sparrows.

Only the brush of so much Armageddon
dusting this sleeve until the dust's my arm,
only so much forewarning becoming provender,
detritus from the banquet of the gods.

Which gods? I ask MySelf, writing this down.
MySelf answers: as if you didn't know!
The ones you woke to when the morning spoke,
the first gods that first breath, and then the next—

Peter Cooley

BILDUNGSROMAN

Because there are stars in the human heart
multiplying there to correspond,
I enter the night to find my apposites—
years on end I go, shine myself back,
my soulmates in darkness come to light.

The stars I'm looking for? They never hide overhead
but underfoot, left, right, diagonal
beneath the step I've left behind or stick
in some live oak up ahead, a scrap of cellophane
prismed by the wind's catapult across the sun.

And then here are the stars—familiars, possible
to count on when I need to count,
Star Mississippi River, Star Lake Pontchartrain.
But I prefer my countlessness: when I look up
the sky's black dome arches, cloudless
vaulted perfected dark.
                    Oh, I have my occupations' thrust
of star-dredging, and constellation-wide
expansion of peripherals, side-on-side on side
swerving—oh, to steady me!—before I sleep.

Peter Cooley

Poem in the Third Week of Advent

And so it is, by resonance of grace
in my soul's eye, through the vision of darkness,
between moonset and sunrise, they begin
again
their journey from eternity, the three
again,
indivisible in imagination.

The Magi imagine me. And God is being born.

Mornings like these, I stand up to myself.
I ask the day for blessings as they come
again,
once more in these trees' obeisance as I pass
beneath them on my morning walk, bowing.

Maybe just one of them will choose me, scatter
the light they never question down the small fire I carry,
their light that gathers at the tops of trees.
The Three Kings setting out. That eternity.
Again.

Derek Otsuji

An Errand Interrupted

If there had been an errand, it was lost to me now
    and the time lost, too, as the part of me that does the thinking
        and attending was waylaid by a single flower falling

from the branch of a pink tacoma, a tissuey blossom tossed
    from a high bough like a handkerchief from the deck
        of a passenger ship at departing, and I thought the sound

it made as it fell was like weeping as another flower
    followed after another, till the fallen blossoms dappled
        the lawn with loose patches of color as in an impressionist

painting, though I could see at the edges of the petals
    that the color was already fading, but the flowers kept
        floating downward in their easeful twirling, as to a courtly

saraband, and looking up into that cloud of boughs
    whose white flurry seemed to hush all sound of the river
        of traffic even then as it rushed beside me, instead of weeping,

I heard laughing and the airy mystery of mirth,
    as I saw that the tree would go on with its giving
        even though nothing but the unlaced fingers of grass

were there to receive it, until the last flower had fallen
    and the branches hung in the air where they shone
        clean as a cross beam, bare in the heaven's blue light.

Christopher Buckley

Yo me perdono

> *Yo me perdono da saber*
> *lo poco que supe in mi vida*
>   –Pablo Neruda

The still stars swirl . . . what can I do
      about the minutes
that keep moving like fish in the sea?
      There must be
a net in the glaze of galaxies that stops time,
      each thought and
memory blurred as starlight, still spinning?
      It doesn't take much
to pause and think, and come up with nothing
      but the empty space
between stars. I contribute so little
      to the landfill now
that I could lift my arms from any bench
      in the park and call out
No. No. Not me. Look—my hands are empty!
      I have only these
indifferent phrases filched from the faded blue,
      leaves of the coral trees
climbing hand over hand up the dark, stars shooting
      past my fingertips,
redshifted, moving away as fast as they can.
      How much has changed
out there, really, over the last millennia?
      I understood so little
about any of this for so long until I forgave myself
      each night, once
I realized how short eternity is here on earth.

Todd Davis

FISHING WITH MY SEVENTEEN-YEAR-OLD SELF

We wade upstream, where light marks the passage
of time, open and forgiving, so when rain begins,
wind and thunder growling over the peak
whose base forms the foundation of this stream,
we're more surprised than scared. A game trail leads us
into a willow-thicket, spit of rock and dirt pushed up
by hundred-year floods, a small island with moving water
on all sides, water also moving from darker skies.
Stuffed full of young aspen and alder, limbs and leaves
lay tight as shingles on a roof, and here in our green hovel,
dry and comfortable, we rest, backs propped on slender trunks,
eyes closed, listening to what now seems far-off weather.
The arterial thrush of the river grows, and when I open
my eyes, your face glistens, faint nimbus exposing the first
evidence of moustache and chin-beard. You're still
young enough to sleep anywhere, and my own old
worries have receded as a softer wind pushes clouds,
slivers of sun beginning to unspool wet branches, a returned
warmth to hatch flies and kingfisher riling the air
with their clicking mantra, a bear rustling willow shoots
fifty yards downstream. But rather than wake you
and go back to tempting cutthroat with figured lines,
I decide to wait a bit longer, to shelter in this country,
the same way I pressed leaves in a book as a boy, hoping
to save what is here and what may yet be.

Peter Leight

SELF-PORTRAIT AS A PASSENGER ON A TRIP

When I think about where I'm going it's almost always somewhere
else, as in a coloring book where you don't even stay between the lines.
Letting my tongue peek out, standing with my head in the sky like
a passenger—it's important not to be loyal, not overly loyal, loyalty
is a form of autopilot. When somebody asks me how far I'm going I
tell her *all the way,* is there any other way? It doesn't mean we're not
getting along with each other, not at all, there isn't that much difference
between longing and needing to move along. Wrapping myself up
in the kind of woolly fleece that insulates completely, even when it's
damp, when I lower one side the other lifts up like a boxtop, breathing
first on one side and then on the other like a swimmer, it doesn't mean
we're traveling together, traveling on the same trip. I'm not taking
anything with me except what I need—I'm thinking of Gene Kelly
running around in Paris with a small cardboard suitcase, holding onto
the handle with his hand curved around the handle, is there anything
inside? I don't have any *reservations* in the sense of appointments made
in advance or reluctance to go any further. Not looking for a stopping
place, not even pausing to take a closer look, it doesn't mean we're not
holding onto each other, perhaps our lips are touching, the emotional
distance is difficult to measure. Of course it's a stress test—I'm taking
a couple of aspirins first. Not lying down together, it's too hard to
get up. When somebody asks me where I am I tell her *on the way*, I
often take the long way around, it's not tiring, not at all, I'm not even
pausing to rest, not even stopping until I don't even know where I
am: it's not an exhibit where you look at something and then move
on to something else. I'm not thinking *I'm coming back to this later.*
I'm actually strengthening, holding onto my waist where the fabric is
gathered under the waistband, as long as I hold on it's going to do what
I want, it's coming with me.

Carol Schaechterle

CONSIDER THE OPOSSUM

No creature so perfectly fitted
to creekside swale and bracken of dried poke
forest as this ghost-faced obsidian–
eyed Opossum, she of the vocative
name, of four strong thumbs and prehensile tail.
Her knobbed toes and flat black feet, arthritic,
ridged, and plated like her tail with bony scales
overlaid, so suited to the scuffing
of February snow or clambering
among the low branches of pines, her mouse–
colored shoulders hunched against Ohio's
wintry blast. Rat-tailed, high-haunched, cleanly,
but no fussy eater, she relishes
nuts and eggs, fruit, insects, small birds and mice,
or, gourmandizing, snails and mushrooms, frogs—
whatever comes her way. She's Midwestern–
polite and just as willing to be pleased.

Plump in her furs, pinch-nosed and just a bit
ridiculous, she's never been a fit
topic for philosopher or poet.
One wants to make more of one's subject
than she allows for. Scientists know her
for her weak placenta, pouch, thrice-yearly
estrus and troubling double vagina—
best not to think toward what pleasing
instrument it shaped itself. She holds
such children as she has room for
in her pouch or else they cling
along her black-tipped hairy sides and back
until they drop, then forage for themselves.
Threaten her; she hisses, showing rat teeth,
or drops still and with profound flatulence

makes her case. Stay, hunter! Leave her be, dogs!
Let her mind her solitary business.

M J Werthman White

I Ask the Dog

Because the answers my human cohort offer are so unsatisfactory,
I've begun addressing questions to the dog. *What can we do, yellow dog?*
The rainforest burns; California is on fire. She stretches, nose to tail tip,
maybe six feet of *I don't know* standing in front of me. I try again.

What about the virus, resembling nothing so much as a depth charge,
presently trying to blow us out of the water? Her yawn makes a little
squeak.

She lies down and rolls over. I scratch her belly saying, *Sorry, am I*
boring you? Does the hole we've dug ourselves into not interest you at all?
She perks up at the mention of "hole" and "dig." I continue, *How to*
stop the hate? How to beat AK47's into plowshares? How begin to love our
neighbors,

especially the ones we don't even like? Yellow dog tentatively, delicately,
licks the back of the hand that feeds her. It's not much; it will have to
be enough.

Melissa Madenski

ODE TO BLACK

Curl on a mallard's tail.
Crow. Raven. Rook.

Size 2 rubber boots.
Non-slip soles. Umbrellas. Raincoats.

The blinding between turning off
a porchlight and the eye's adjustment.

Roots. Dirt. Echinacea seeds,
black-eyed Susan. What the night needs.

Turtle neck sweaters. Herbie Hancock jazz.

Feathers. Ouzels/Dippers.
Kingfisher's eye ring. Chickadees cap.
Townsend Warbler's stripes.

Sea Lion flippers.

Black Bear. Wood duck's mullet.
Leather-winged bats.

Beetles.

Lantern gone cold.
Candle snuffed.
Coals.

Boats erased in the pre-dawn river. Prow lights
bobbing like balloons untethered.

Night flight over unlit fields.

Black Lives Matter signs.
Black letters on tape stretched across
downtown streets. Rights. Might.

One cloud behind the mountain.
One tree in the park.
One confluence of creeks rushing to merge.

The absence of light.
The engine sparking stars.

Emily Jennings

BIRDS

The tree rains tiny yellow birds, dying
As they land on shriveled ground after long
Winding dissents in all directions but
Headed downward to nothing and faded
Brown. The corpses crumble loud underfoot
And rains dissolve them as acid dissolves,
Slowly. These finches flitted from branch to
Nest, nervous, anticipating the worst.
And the worst came, as it does, with a frost
And a strong wind from the north, the first day
Of November. I trample the exposed
Graves walking to my mailbox, shivering.

David Ricchiute

A Daughter's Conviction

*The female weavers assembled in parliament, to the
number . . . of one hundred and two . . . The result . . . was a resolution
to abandon their looms. —Providence Journal, May 31, 1824*

No less sudden than a shooting star,
she rose, this daughter of a fate foretold,
young but nameless in the records that survive,
including the diaries of weaving-mill barons
—each an owner of a breathtaking mansion
none of the mill-weavers dared tread near—

to lead one hundred & one other women,
bleeding from wear to fingers & hands,
the first in history to rise together
in a walk-off-the-shop-floor labor strike,
absent men too timid at first

to turn from their mechanized weaving looms
to the exits of wood-frame textile mills
in defiance of the area's merchant barons,
who'd ordered a 20-percent cut in wages
& an hour longer to a too-long day.

Who are *you* who took the reins, daughters
of the mothers of the Revolution, mothers
of the daughters who'd turn suffragettes,
the models I told my daughter about
to re-enact in a grade-school sketch

—Susan B. Anthony, Ida B. Wells—
before she probed for herself far deeper,
before she discovered the textile weavers

who still, to this day, remain unnamed
but have everything to do

with my daughter's conviction
to join in union with like-minded sisters,
traveling by foot on foreign soil
to care for the children of ailing patients
too feeble to care for the children themselves.

The ones unnamed, unknown, she said.
The ones in the mills two centuries ago.
Sisters, my sisters, with the children now
—the daughters to tell our daughters about,
their young blood risen for a cause that lands.

Joan Seliger Sidney

French-Knot Flowers

Across my lap, a new tapestry. A village scene
Its church steeple gold, sunlight spilling
Onto the street. In front farmers
Scythe fields of deep purple grapes.
Two draft horses pull the wagon field
To field as children stand, stomp bare feet
To speed wine-making. It could be
A scene from Baden. It could be me
At thirteen in the wagon while Mother
And Grandmother took the Baths. If only
They were still alive to see me stitch.
I reach for my embroidery
Needle and silk thread. They
Taught me everything
From simple cross-stitching
To French-knot flowers. I'll
Begin with the running stitch to outline
The design, then the stem stitch for vines,
The satin stitch to fill in leaves.
Voices. Neighbors and shopkeepers
Stand on the sidewalk, joking. A peddler's
Cart of oranges perfumes my room.
I can almost taste the sweet sections, almost
Feel the juice run down my chin. If not
For needing to keep the tapestry clean, I'd
Call down and ask him to bring up two or three.
I see men on their knees
Scrub the sidewalk
With their beards. Such variety:
Long and thin like dirty thread.
A wash of colors tinged
With gray, thick bushes of black
Or brown or even a flash
Of red. But how can I concentrate?

Those shrieks from the street
Worse than cats in heat screeching,
Jolt my steady hand.

Roger Camp

Mr. Lucky Goes to Market

for Doug Larson

In the television series, *Mr. Lucky,*
the title character is played by John Vivyan,
a gambler whose wins include
the yacht-based casino he operates.
In real life, Mr. Lucky is played
by my more mundane self.
On TV, Mr. Lucky's wristwatch
chimes with the first five notes
of the series' theme,
Mancini's hit melody,
sounding a shaken, not stirred note of cool.
No fool, my Mr. Lucky is the guy
who gets the last parking space
in front of the bank
or the customer the market cashier beckons
to the register she just opened.
No fortunes won or lost on the flop
but a smattering of small pats
spread like sweet butter
over a lifetime
invoking my grandfather's remark:
if you're lucky, you don't have to be smart,
this from the man
who with gold coins sewn
in the armpits of his shirt
walked five hundred miles
across the Mesopotamian desert
escaping with his life
from a Turkish death march.

Brandon Krieg

ONE FOR WHALEN

Pump filter broke
on the steep ascent
above Top Spur.
Mobbed by horseflies,
I boiled water cup by
cup. She, passing, offered
iodine, I took instead
envy of her lying
among huge boulders
above the timberline
watching the Perseids alone.
Later, I shared the sake I carried
with two Danes
camped nearby, hid from winds
blowing dust under
the rainfly of my tent, the cover
of my *Book of Job* gritty
as I read. "Job took it in stride"
the introduction said,
words I chewed to sleep.
Woke among the volcanoes,
crossed August-low forks
of Hood River on slick bark-less
trunks others dropped across.
The alpine meadow pond
from lost Junes, Julys
dried into a ring
of ultragreen grass. No shade
in the scorched forest
on the north side, the trees
standing branchless, silver-dead.
Less than rest, I needed
to feel uncapturable
distances as deep ache

in thighs. Later, exhausted,
crossing the highest snowfield,
my mind swirled habitual
angers, boiling like glacier water
I was forced to drink hot
on the baking rocks—
winter storms melted to feed
storms in me. They fed, too,
the White River
where Whalen fished
in a poem with his father.
I dipped my undershirt
in its silty wash, pulled it back on,
and ambled up the last
grueling switchbacks of blowing
volcanic dust, feeling it
cool against my skin.

Keith Morris

You're a Damned Pile of Dust

For RKP

I saw you
talked to you
a thousand times.

I sat on your couch
listened to The Beatles with you
"How does it feel to be one of the beautiful people?"

I laughed with you
You consoled me when I hurt
You hugged me. Remember?

You were ALWAYS there
Here
Present

I remember.
I recreate

Now,
your oldest daughter points to a
pot on a shelf
in a closet where you reside.

A welder's cap half-covering an ocean-colored ceramic shape
and that's you now.

I guess I'm crazy as I sit here now, just talking away to you like you're sitting
    right there.
I'll never, never admit you're there.

Sheryl Massaro

PRECIPITATION

I recall sitting in rain
that fell through sunlight,
and driving in rain
that made roads
disappear. The first
would be the Female
Rain, and the second
the Male Rain, as our
native people say.
I recall impervious ice,
the hail-cracked windshields
of Saskatchewan,
racing down snowy hills
on saucers, pungent
woolens burdened
with burrs of snow.
I recall walking
through early winter,
through the scent
of woodsmoke,
through the delicate
cold touch of the first
stars of snow
melting into skin.

Sheryl Massaro

THE WATER TASTING

She knelt at one end
of the long table
so that only one side
of the first bottle
was visible,
and then she shifted
to the left
in increments,
so that each next bottle
slowly came into view,
prisms at their feet
from the warm sun
behind them.

So went her ritual
at every tasting
to keep her from taking
these waters for granted.
So many, from so many places,
each a magical fluid.

She would not be today's
only water sommelier.
There always were a few,
each bearing a keen eye,
the nose of a bloodhound,
discerning tastebuds,
an exquisite thirst.

They could taste rock
earth minerals textures
sweetness saltiness
umami in waters
from everywhere.

filtered through mountains,
siphoned from deep layers
of freshwater Ice Age melt
that sank and stayed
on the ocean floor,
the thaws of glaciers,
the cores of icebergs,
groundwaters, rain,
bubbly, still.

To perch on this table,
a water must be raw,
untouched, unpurified,
thousands of years old.
It must be respected
by the locals,
who are its protectors,
drink it daily,
claim healing or miracles
or blue zone lifespans
for generations.

Hype. A miracle healing,
the Romans bathed here,
from a secret sacred
Polynesian spring,
the purest water from
the heart of ancient ice
that is no more. She knew
her ribbon would go
to the crisp Italian,
the one who did best
the magic of all waters.

The taste of the terroir
of each selection.

Kristen Roach

Amish Love Song

Black hat, black horse, black wheels. Turn round
to marry me with bridle rings
and mark this mud as holy ground.

A blond-curled boy, you once were bound
in blue suspenders, apron strings,
and hat. Black horse, black wheels turn round–

the reins in hands the sun has browned
in wheat field autumns, bean sprout springs,
that mark this mud as holy ground.

Your silence is my favorite sound.
I pray each time your buggy brings
your hat and horse; my wheels turn round.

On Sundays, all my breath unwound,
I stand with you and gasp to sing
and mark this mud as holy ground.

Let's build our barn, let hammers pound,
like hearts and hooves and rising wings.
Black hat, black horse, black wheels turn round
and mark this mud as holy ground.

Ken Holland

Rapture

It's that time of year when the hawk must think it
A sudden feast, the mindless flaying of the trees
From a storm just passed

> Leaves freshly stripped; carrion exposed
> Like a woman dressed in chiffon.

> Held aloft, this last moment before trespass,
> Before the wind allows for descent

And then descent itself.

See how we follow

How we too have something sharp about the mouth,
Something capable of rending

The way our arms spread out as if to embrace
What's holy, illuminated.

And there, in the bright splay of leaf-fall,
Just within reach of the edge of our talon

> Right there

> Carrion.

Ken Holland

An Interrupted Treatise on Domestic Tranquility

I think I'm finally getting a handle on the concept
Of marital bliss, except there's an early nor'easter
Pummeling through and there's nothing I can do
To get out the door, the snow's already banked
Deep enough to take my mind away from all
I've failed at, how there isn't enough scrap paper
To write it all down, not with the light wasting away,
It's not just the darkness of the storm but the power's been out
Two hours now and I'm thankful for the quilts
My wife left me when she herself left me,
Also a fry pan and a pot big enough to boil water in,
And here's the snow piling high up against the window,
Beautiful in its depth, the storm itself a quilt
That's tucked up against the neck of the house
And I think I'll have one more pour of brandy
For the good it does my blood, for its sifting embers
Of self-pity, shamed though I am to take on such warmth,
But show me the dog that won't curl up to a fire
Or prick his ears when the wind skirls higher and higher.

Luke Wallin

An Elephant Might

He was watching the night when he suddenly asked
the universe whole, entire,

Do you know I'm you, become conscious?

Can you awaken to my language?

Are you so beautiful and so large, mother of fractals,
ever expanding, without awareness, except in me?

Do you wonder what I mean?
Do you know me the way an elephant might?

Are you like my child who hasn't spoken to me, now seven years?
Or like the crows in my field, who know a sort of me?

If all is determined, was I on your unconscious mind all along?

Do you relish blowing out my candle?
Or is the span of my life short for you, as for me?

Will you grieve when we are gone?
Will you replay our hologram?

Will you be like an old man, remembering, still loving his wife?

K. J. Bundy

Dream House

We were in the piney kitchen of his grandparents' house, the knots in the wood like dark eyes. The matching avocado appliances and calico curtains bravely enduring the reek of stale beer. I was about to tell Teddy I was leaving him when the doorbell rang and The Queen was inside, fresh from church and dressed in a raw silk dress. His father shuffled in behind, tie loosened, watching golf highlights on his phone.

"Teddy, what's going on here?" she asked, her blue blood rising. The white velvet sofa in the living room was streaked with orange handprints, and a half-empty bag of Cheetos sat on the coffee table. It made my stomach flip, because I knew from his grandmother's diary the sofa was the first big furniture purchase his grandparents ever made.

"Mom, I'll clean it up," Teddy said, pinching his eyes.

His father looked up from his phone and muttered, "Oh for God's sake, Son." I took the crumpled bag to the kitchen, picturing Teddy gorging himself in the wee hours of the morning while I was upstairs dreaming his grandparents and I were having Sunday roast together.

I moved in with Teddy two months ago, but I'd never told him about my dreams. How sometimes I'd find myself stringing green beans with his grandmother or playing checkers with his grandfather, things she wrote about in her diary. Who knew there were people who built houses from Sears kits and matching playhouses in the backyard for the kids? People who sat down at the kitchen table together every night for dinner, television off.

"Kayla will get this cleaned up, right?" The Queen said in a low voice, and my hands shook as I tried to stuff the Cheetos bag into a trash can overflowing with beer cans. After she found out Granny raised me in a one-bedroom apartment, she told Teddy that's why I liked rearranging the furniture and trying out all his grandmother's recipes.

Playing house, she called it. And when Teddy told her I found his grandmother's diary she said, "Well of course she found it. She's nosy about our kind of people. Wishes she could be like us."

She is one dangerous bitch, that Queen.

I could hear them talking about going out for brunch and I knew then I was going to leave, was absolutely going to leave this time, and

I hurried downstairs. His grandparents were stationed in Hawaii after they got married and she asked him to build a tiki bar in their rec room to remind her of their time there. They liked to dance to Don Ho music down here after the children had gone to bed. I took a picture of the bar with my phone, then picked up a tiny framed photo of his grandparents and slid it in my pocket. When I got upstairs, the three of them were standing together in a clump in front of the sofa, The Queen reapplying her lipstick, his father looking at his phone, Teddy rubbing his temples. I touched my jeans, felt the edges of the photo frame, and hoped they couldn't see it. I told them I wasn't going to brunch. A blood vessel under my left eye began pulsing and I wondered if they noticed. She cocked her head and said *why in the world not*, and the throbbing grew stronger.

I said we needed a break, and Teddy's face crumbled. My throat tightened and I was about to apologize just to get us through the moment, then caught myself. At first I loved him, loved waking up next to him under the pink chenille bedspread on his grandparents' bed. And then I didn't, mainly because of the drinking, but also because he didn't respect the house which meant he didn't respect his grandparents. Who deserved better.

The Queen reached out to grab me and I wondered later if she was so happy I was leaving she was trying to hug me. In the moment though, I wasn't entirely sure, so I pushed her, not hard, but hard enough that she fell backward onto the white sofa. As she was going down I could see a tiny line of silver in the part of her hair, like a little piece of truth, and the room began spinning. The ticking under my eye was out of control now, and I wondered if a vein was rupturing under my skin.

Teddy and his father scrambled to help her, and I grabbed my backpack and escaped out the back, the screen door slamming behind me. I stumbled across the backyard, gulping in air, running toward the playhouse which was now hidden behind a row of overgrown boxwood bushes.

Yellowed linen curtains, made from remnants his grandmother found at her favorite fabric store, billowed when I opened the little door. There were kitchen cupboards his grandfather built from the same knotty pine, and child-sized plastic dishes and cups in a drainer next to a sink. I collapsed on a twin bed topped by a frayed, floral quilt, and tried not to think about Teddy's quivering chin, the flash of silver.

Playing house.

I breathed in the tang of the wood and the old cotton inside the quilt, and when a bloom of sunlight spilled through the windows, I felt my chest soften. The room glowed and for just a second I let myself be here as a little girl, washing the tiny dishes and carefully placing them in the drainer.

And then tree branches outside the windows rose and a cloud passed in front of the sun, turning everything inside cool and gray. I felt for the tiny picture in my pocket, the edges pressing hard against my thigh, the sterling frame now warm. I pulled it out and as I stood to leave dropped it on the quilt, wondering why I thought it belonged to me, why I ever thought any of it might belong to me.

D. A. Becher

Doors

The metal door opened in front of me, beckoning me to a new life. The words of my old high school teacher, Ms. Heskamp, from some ten years before echoed in my head.

"I hope that you are considering college and where you might want to go. With your grades and intelligence, I just know you'd knock the socks off the SAT's. The test is in a couple months and I noticed you haven't signed up to take it yet, so I thought we could talk a bit about your plans."

Ms. Heskamp sat across her desk from me. I was seated in a wooden chair in front of her. Ms. Heskamp was a petite woman with grey hair worn in a short-cropped bob. She had glasses she only used to read dangling on a chain around her neck. She divided her time at my high school between teaching English and counseling. Her watery, pale blue eyes gazed at me while she waited for my response.

We had read the novel *Christy* in her English class—a work about a woman who moved to the Smoky Mountain community of Cutter Gap to work with impoverished Appalachian children. Ms. Heskamp explained to the students in the class that she had been motivated by *Christy* to move to our eastern Kentucky community of Coleton from Cincinnati, Ohio in the late 70's following her graduation from Mount St. Joseph College. She said she wanted to "make a difference." This did not make much of an impression on us, since most of us did not feel ourselves to be impoverished. Many of our dads worked in the coal industry—miners, mine equipment repairmen, railroad workers, and the like. They made good money—especially in the union jobs.

After a long pause I slowly spoke. "No offense ma'am, but I don't particularly want to go to college. My boyfriend's uncle is a section boss at a union mine and has told Jimmy, that's my boyfriend, that after he graduates Jimmy can get a good job there. We'll get married and have two or three kids. I plan to be the perfect wife and mama. I really don't care to go to school anymore after I graduate from here."

I could see a visceral look of disappointment in her face that almost made me ashamed of what I had said. "Tina dear," she said softly, "there are choices in life that open doors and choices that close doors that may never be opened again. I know that is what you think now but consider 20 years from now; you may wonder what your life could have been."

I could feel my face flush. "Ms. Heskamp, I *consider* that I will be a mother and grandmother, with my kids stopping in to talk with me, grandkids on my knees, Sundays with everyone over for dinner in a nice house my husband bought for us. I do not *consider* that I will be old and alone with no family close by to take care of and comfort me," I almost hissed out through clenched teeth, knowing that she would know that I spoke of her.

It was her turn for a change in face color—ashen. It appeared that she might be choking back tears when she finally managed to say, "I am sorry my dear, we all get to make our own choices in life and then must live with them no matter what the consequences. You're free to go."

I stalked out the door, slamming it shut as I went. I sought out my best friend, Mary Hensley, in the school cafeteria. I stormed over to her in a rage. "I can't believe that Ms. Heskamp wants to run my life. Where the heck does she get off!"

"Why, what's the matter?" Mary asked.

"She wants to make me feel like a fool for wanting to marry Jimmy and settle down with him here. She wants to have me run off to college somewhere; leave Jimmy who is just bound to find someone else if I go—looking like he does from all that weightlifting for football, with a great job lined up! I just couldn't go off and lose him."

"You are the smartest girl in the class—gonna be valedictorian I'll bet," Mary said. "Ms. Heskamp just wants to look out for you."

"Let her look out for herself, the old bitch!"

"Tina Thatcher, I can't believe you said that! What would Reverend Atkins say?"

"Don't care," I said. "I don't want to wind up a lonely old spinster like her. I got a plan that will make certain Jimmy and I stay together here—in Coleton—with my family all around and us making our own family."

"What you gonna do?"

"Well, you know I've been telling you how Jimmy is getting friskier and friskier. Putting his hands down my shirt and lately down my pants too. It feels pretty good, but I've always stopped him from going any further; although I've kinda helped him, uh, find release with my hands on his thing."

Mary blushed, "Bet the Reverend doesn't know that about you two."

"We love each other, so I don't see any harm in it. Anyway, I figure I'm gonna start letting Jimmy go further—see my boobs and maybe other things. Prom is coming up and I'll be midway between my periods, so . . . ."

"Oh my God!" Mary exclaimed, "You wanna get pregnant."

"Well why not? He says he wants to marry me and have a family. Why would God care if we wait a few months or do it now. Jimmy's starting work at the mine right after graduation. This might speed things up a bit, but it'll make sure all this talk of leaving for college, or for anywhere else, is put to rest."

Yup, that was the plan I hatched. A little stereotypical but, if they hadn't already, so many girls in my high school lost their virginity on prom night that it was almost a tradition—although most at least made their boyfriends use condoms. I left that part out. And my plan worked. I missed my period, took the pregnancy test, told Jimmy, broke the good/bad news to our parents and we were married within the month by Reverend Atkins.

Jimmy did get that good job at the mine. We lived at first at Jimmy's parents' house with our new baby. But it was not long before we rented our own place. A second baby came and Jimmy made enough that we bought a pre-fab house. My dad gave us a piece of ground to put it on in the holler where he lived.

In our area of Appalachia, a holler (actually spelled hollow) is a narrow valley running up into the mountains a ways; usually with a small stream or creek down the middle. Dad's dad had originally bought the strip of land forming the holler. Dad and Uncle Dan had both been given land in the holler by grandpa. Uncle Dan had already carved off two pieces of his to give to a son and a daughter. I was the first of my siblings to get married. There would not be enough ground for my sister and two brothers, but dad said he figured that maybe their future spouses' parents would give them some land or one of them might move off somewhere up north like Cincinnati or Dayton. He said all he cared about right then was having his two grandkids close by.

Things went along pretty well for a while: A third baby, being able to visit dad and mom whenever I wanted. It was pretty much the life I'd planned for myself. Then more and more often Jimmy began to go out for drinks after work. He'd come home smelling of beer and fall asleep in his chair every night watching TV. I just went into the bedroom and closed the door so as not to hear his snoring.

He began to get, well . . . a bit flabby. I put on quite a bit of weight after the third kid that I just could not get rid of. With Jimmy's drinking and falling asleep, and I suppose both of us not looking as hot as we once did, our love making became more and more infrequent and perfunctory. When he did share my bed, he'd climb on top of me, do his business, roll over, and then fall asleep snoring at a crescendo that made it impossible for me to sleep. When this happened, I'd spend the night crashed out on the couch closing the bedroom door behind me.

"Where in the hell have you been?" I asked Jimmy one night when he didn't come home until 9:30.

"After I cleaned up at the bath-house I stopped for a beer at the bar. Decided to order a burger and got in an interesting conversation. Sorry about that," he said with no hint of sincerity as he headed to bed, loudly slamming the door behind him.

That's how it began; him more often than not coming home late. When I asked him where he'd been, he'd repeat the same old mantra, "Just stopped in for a burger and a beer and got to talking."

One day I thought, *Things have got to change. This is not the way it's supposed to be.* Finally. I decided, *If you want things to change, you've got to do something to change them.* The phrase, *Well, if you can't lick 'em, join 'em,* came to mind. I wandered over to my mom's on a Tuesday and asked if the kids could have a sleep-over the next night.

She was a bit curious, "What, on a school night?"

"Yeah, I want to go out with Jimmy, and there are some Wednesday night specials at the Dew Drop Inn." Sometimes I think half the bars in eastern Kentucky adopted that overused moniker. (I know what you're thinking, but I do use words like "moniker"—valedictorian, remember.) Since it was the only bar/restaurant in town, it was not hard to figure out where Jimmy was stopping.

"Well okay!" she enthusiastically responded. "I was kinda thinking that you and Jimmy weren't getting along too well these days. Glad to hear it. Your dad will be delighted to have the grandkids here."

I didn't tell her that I planned on it being a surprise for Jimmy. I truly thought I needed to start spending more time with him away from home, and I could chug down longnecks as well as anybody. It might not be the best activity to do together—but I figured it was a start.

I got to the Dew Drop at about 6:30 p.m. It had been, what . . .

                                          The Louisville Review

almost two years since I had been in the place. It had a menu that could best be described as bar food. No beer on tap—just bottles and cans. I stood at the door hesitating a few seconds, wondering if maybe I should have actually made plans with Jimmy—but I did want it to be a surprise. Nothing ventured, nothing gained as they say. I opened the door. I looked around at the tables and booths, with their cracked red vinyl benches and chairs. No Jimmy. There were several men at the old beer stained bar, but no Jimmy.

Then I wandered around the corner and saw the door to a room that I recalled held a pool table and a couple of card tables with folding chairs. I began to push on it very slowly and discretely as possible; I didn't want to embarrass Jimmy if he was playing pool with some co-workers. It seemed someone had placed a chair behind it, but I continued to push it just enough to see into the room.

After peering in for a bit, I noticed two people in chairs at the far end of the room where you could barely see due to the dim light. There Jimmy sat talking to a red head seated next to him. I finally recognized her as Patty Pearson—a cheerleader from Jimmy's football glory days. I at first thought that she'd just stopped in for a drink and they struck up a conversation about old high school times—could not figure out the chair against the door though.

I saw Jimmy whisper in her ear. She giggled, moved closer, and engaged in an obvious tongue in the mouth passionate kiss. Evidently, they assumed they were alone and unwatched, because her hand moved down to his belt, she undid it and unzipped his jeans. I quietly closed the door, turned, and rapidly left the building through the front door.

I drove home navigating through the tears in my eyes. I sat in the living room thinking. The thinking turned into plotting. After a couple trips between the garage and our bedroom, I lay down on the couch and closed my eyes. At about 10 o'clock Jimmy came in and I assume saw me and thought I was asleep, for he headed straight to the bedroom. I waited for his snoring to begin and got up. I took the 2 x 4 I had ready and braced one end under the doorknob of the bedroom door. I took Jimmy's cordless drill and some screws and screwed the opposite end into the floor; just like I had screwed them into the window frames of the bedroom. Jimmy's rhythmic snoring continued.

I opened the door to the garage and lifted a gas can that I had placed next to it, poured gas under the door to the bedroom, and trailed gas behind me to the front door. I opened the front door, struck a match and lit a book of matches from our wedding reception. Just before I exited the front door, I tossed the flaming matches into the gasoline. I closed and locked it—didn't want any do-gooders or first-responders to be able to quickly enter. Besides, I wanted the door to that part of my life permanently closed.

After I had passed through the entrance, the metal door to the maximum-security wing of the Kentucky Correctional Institution for Women clanged shut behind me. Life in prison with no parole. *Ms. Heskamp, I almost chuckled, *you were right; some closed doors just won't be reopening for me.*

Elmo Lum

BEAUTIFUL

I haven't felt any good in many weeks. There's been a bug making the rounds that I caught early on in the season, the exact wrong time of the season, because I was still working a job. It's bad this year, the bug, and it put me down for days and days when I couldn't afford to set aside any days. Then, by the time I came to, they'd already replaced me on the job, and that didn't leave me enough money to swap out the tires on my truck. So of course, one of them blew, and then patching it cost me a chunk of change, so again the year is turning over and again I'm flat broke. I've been trading in electrical work down at George's for food and fuel, but the bigwigs there frown on enterprise, so we've been keeping the deal hush-hush. If I didn't know the night manager, I'd be starving and freezing my ass this winter. Another gut-starving and ass-freezing winter.

Plus, yesterday the beautiful people drove through, perched in their vans and SUVs, weaving the lanes and potholes of town: another Daughter's Day. Which is damn near worthless to me, since I've got no daughter and no son, but especially because I haven't got a daughter. Not to mention they kill jobs for us, because—while they like to spruce everything up—the beautiful people bring in their own help, which leaves us locals out in the cold. Which means I probably won't find much work until springtime, at least the way this winter's been unraveling for me so far.

The beautiful people made a pass through town, then circled back again; by now we'd lined the main drag (myself included, even though I've never had a daughter). The second time through they stopped and stepped from their vans to pass out bananas and grapefruit to the throngs of us (myself included—I haven't peeled a banana in years). From the high school came running daughters, smoothing their hips and snugging their ponytails, baring thighs and shoulders and navels though their skin was stippling from the cold. Behind them, resting hands on their shoulders, came mothers from (usually) George's, still dressed as greeters and cashiers, preening themselves along with their daughters. We men (myself included) got crowded to the rear, as is usual for us men for Daughter's Day.

To the girls, the beautiful people passed out compliments along with their fruit. The girls who pushed to the front all bit their lips and chewed their hair. This included the girls who got pushed to the front by their mothers (from, usually, George's); behind them watched the girls too young for Daughter's Day. The younger girls all bit their lips and chewed their hair, too, half-mocking and half-pretending to be their older sisters. The older sisters kept on their smiles until the beautiful people passed, then cussed out the younger girls before shoving them away. Away up the street were the girls who turned up their noses at the whole affair; entirely hidden were the fat girls, the awkwards, the uglies, and the weirds. (I remember from my high school days, before I dropped out, the principal and teachers herding them into the auditorium until the beautiful people drove away.)

Four weeks, said the beautiful people before driving out through the crowd, leaving only enough beautiful people to snap portraits and take down names.

"My mother was once a finalist," confessed Inez. She dragged on one of my cigarettes.

We were in bed. "No kidding," I said.

"No kidding. I guess my mother was a hottie. Back in the day. Isn't that what they used to say? Back in your day?"

"What do they say now?"

"I don't know. Different things. There's not one word that means that now."

"So, are you going to try out?"

Inez blew smoke in my face.

"Your mother want you to try out?"

"I hope not, God. I haven't talked to her. She's been working swing, remember? Anyway, that's not quite up to her. That's not quite up to me. You know that. Don't you always tell me you remember?"

"They still make you try out at school?"

"Of course. If you're not deformed, obese, or weird."

"Maybe you should act weird."

She shook her head. "Even if you're weird, sometimes they still make you try out then."

"Let me take a drag."

Inez didn't give up the cigarette, just held it to my lips. When I pulled away, she took a last pull, then stubbed the butt of it out. "Maybe I should go obese," she said.

"Don't do that. I'm putting my foot down."

"Your foot can go to hell. I could do it."

"In four weeks? You couldn't afford to go obese in ten weeks."

"Maybe my boyfriend will help me out. Buy me lots of ice cream. Gallons and gallons of it. I keep a secret boyfriend, you know."

"Do you? Well, if your boyfriend hails from these parts, he couldn't afford ice cream, either. Ice cream hasn't been sold here for years."

"Oh, yeah. I was eleven years old."

"God, I'm an old man."

"You know, I remember you when I was eleven."

"Get out. Why do you lie, Inez?"

"No, I'm serious. I remember you drove that car."

"What car? Only car I ever drove was my truck."

"Didn't you? I remember this. It was a little two-door convertible, brown, and the top was flaking off. Come to think of it, I guess the brown was flaking off, too."

"I know what you're talking about. That wasn't mine. That was French's. He moved away about that time, when the George's took away his daddy's business."

"I didn't know whose car that was. I just always saw you around it."

"Yeah. That was the only wheels between us. So of course, we were always around it."

"You look the same."

"I don't remember."

"You remember me when I was eleven?"

"What are you saying? I ogled eleven-year-olds?"

"Can I have another cigarette?"

"If you let me smoke some this time."

Inez flicked the cigarette lit, pulled, then fingered it over to me. She blew a plume. "You know, I was a cute eleven-year-old."

"Are you saying you were an eleven-year-old hottie?"

Inez laughed. "They weren't even saying that when I was eleven."

"I am an old man."

"Tell me about it." She took back the cigarette. "So, what I'm hearing is you don't remember me."

"I can't say I do."

"You were just waiting until I reached high school, weren't you?"

"You know it, hottie. I was just biding my time."

Inez laughed and smacked my arm.

"You're ashing on the sheets again, baby."

"Oh, shit." She brushed it out, a gray smear. "Mama's going to be home soon."

"I know."

Inez stood, passed me the cigarette, started to pull on her panties. "You have any gum?"

"You don't?"

"I ran out."

"I might have some left on the dresser."

Inez rummaged. "Last piece."

"Go ahead." I watched the shape of her tug on her pants, hook on her bra, pull her top over her head.

"Mama's got a double coming up on Thursday. See you then?"

"Oh, baby. Two shifts for the price of one."

"You're such a dirty old man." She pulled out her gum to kiss me, then put it back.

"It's important to have goals. They still tell you that at school?"

Inez rolled her eyes. "Yes, God. So, Thursday?"

"With bated breath."

"What?"

"Don't even ask me why I said that. I don't even know what bated is."

Inez zipped up her jacket, smoothed her hair, stepped into her shoes. "Sometimes you're very weird," she said.

They came with paint. They came with nails. They came with spools and spools of wire. They came with light bulbs, they came with tar paper, they came with bags of cement. They brought in new plants for the window boxes, brought in new trees for the street, tore up the sidewalks to dig out the old ones, then planted the new, fresh trees in place. They set out park benches along the sidewalk even though there isn't a park for miles. They broke into the abandoned businesses, filled the windows with outside merchandise. They painted new signs over the old signs, painted new names on the plate glass windows. They put up an awning over Ted's old hardware store, set out tables like for a cafe. Where Sara used to run her mama's diner, they installed a flower shop where the flowers they showed "for sale" were all manufactured from cloth. Where Greta used to do dry cleaning, they cordoned off a staging area (that was what the signs and sawhorses read: "Staging Area." Where Lee used to be the butcher, they installed an espresso joint where the beautiful people were allowed to gather but was off-limits to us. They commandeered roofs and second floor windows for lights, cameras, and equipment. They towed our cars from the main drag to bring in two backhoes armed with jackhammers. To a slow and steady rhythm, they punched a grid of holes in the street, followed after by the milling machine that chewed off the top few inches. The ground-up asphalt was spit off a conveyer and into a waiting dump truck. Then came the pouring of new asphalt, smoothed at first with a crew wielding rakes, then driven over with a roller truck to finish it off. The street was new and black; they painted on crosswalks and center dividers, even hatch marks where you were supposed to park your car.

Last, they put up new signs at both ends of the main drag: the street was to be closed to local traffic for the duration of the shoot. Instead, to run our errands, to get our supplies, to go to work and school, we had to crowd the dusty alleys and rutted side streets. None of us could see the reason we couldn't drive the street in the meantime, so we convinced Dierdre, our mayor, to bring it up with the beautiful people. They told her they'd consider it. They'd hold a meeting, they said. That night they posted guards at each end who perched on stools and crackled walkie-talkies. When winter rained, they put up awnings just big enough for the guard. When the sun came out the guard would move his stool to perch in the sun. According to them, this was a minor inconvenience. According to them, this was a boon. After all, they said, we would be keeping all this once Daughter's Day was finished.

"I'm fucking starving. I'm fucking ravenous. I'm fucking famished," Inez said. "Mama's been starving me and starving me, for weeks for that fucking show."

"Oh, yeah. I forgot about that. But I bet the other girls are starving, too."

"Fuck the other girls. You got something to eat or don't you?"

"Easy, Inez. It won't be gourmet, but I'm sure I've got something around."

"I don't care. I'm fucking starving."

I followed her into the kitchen, watched her tear into a loaf of bread. She gnawed a slice of bread rolled up naked of anything else on it.

"I've probably got fixings for a sandwich."

"Maybe later," muffled Inez through the bread.

"You could toast that, too, you know. I definitely got some butter and I might have some jam."

"Toast, yes," she cottoned through her mouthful. She loaded the toaster with two slices, started chewing up a third. "If the power holds out."

"It will. They always keep everything running through the last day."

I looked in the fridge and it turned out I'd got left a little jam, so I brought it out, set it out on the table, rattled a knife out of the drainer. Inez clattered a dish from the cabinet. Still chewing on the bread, she stood tapping the dish and watching the toaster toast. When the toast dinged up, she plucked the toast with her fingers, saying, "Hot, hot, hot." At the table she spread one slice with jam, then bit a semi-circle out of it. While she chewed, she battered out the last of the jam over her last slice of toast. She bit from one and then the other, each toast held in each one hand. When she finished, she fingered up crumbs from the dish and licked them off her fingers. "I'm still a little bit starving," she said.

"There's more," I said.

"You're out of jam."

"I meant other things."

"I know. I ate all your jam."

"I didn't even know I had jam left."

"Well, now you don't."

"I guess that's true. You want something else?"

"Maybe later. Mama's working another double."

"I know. You told me. I've been counting on it."

"I know you've been counting on it." She stood to give me a kiss.

"You taste like jam."

"That's such a lie. Taste me again."

I kissed her again.

Inez said, "That's not the way I meant it."

I said, "Give me some credit. I hear you speaking in code. I'm just doing the first thing before the next thing."

The last time I saw a Daughter's Day I was about to drop out of high school, and when I was about to drop out of high school, half the girls were just like Inez: at least when their mothers weren't looking, they were sarcastic eye-rollers who whispered behind cupped hands about the other half of the girls. About the ones who threw themselves into the fray: the primpers and preeners, the hair-sprayers and mini-skirters, the girls who laid their plans to make it out of our jerkwater town. The ones who looked ahead, who wrote down goals like they teach you in high school, etched over and over in ballpoint pen on their binders: *Get out of this jerkwater town.*

Thursday was slotted for Daughter's Day, so by the following Wednesday (said the beautiful people) they could have the film edited and ready for broadcast nationwide. Right up until that last week, Inez's mother worked double shifts to make up for the ones she traded in to help Inez get beautiful that week. Up until that last week, right up through Sunday night, Inez came over, ravenous, eating, then screwing, then sometimes eating again. She was starting to carve a dent in my wallet, plus I'd been calling in favors at George's, so I was relieved at least by half when Monday finally rolled around. After that, I knew I wouldn't see Inez again until after Daughter's Day, what with her mother watching her every minute and every move.

A stage was erected at one end of the drag along with shining, green bleachers that the beautiful people told us ahead of time weren't going to be for us. On the bleachers and lining the street, they'd arranged to bring in extras from out of town to play the folk (that's how we were called now: the "folk").

Said the pageant director: "We'd love to have you folk be there to cheer on your daughters, but to get that television verisimilitude, we need people who can take direction. And as much as we'd love to have you—and as much as I'd love to have you—we just don't have the time to train you for it. Arrangements have been made to set up seating on one of the rooftops over there for any and all who want to watch. And I promise: we'll pick a good rooftop, won't we?"

That's what she said on Tuesday. Come Wednesday morning came the darkening sky, come lunchtime came the prickly air, come afternoon came the rush of hammering rain. The beautiful people went frantic, ducking their shoulders beneath their clipboards as they ran to unplug the stage lights, shade the catering, tarp the cameras. They'd just been ready to start their dry run as they called it, where they coached the girls through their motions just before the big day. The girls weren't all dressed or painted up, but they huddled under awnings anyway, holding their scripts (or directions, or whatever they were clutching) in umbrellas over their heads. I'd managed to swing work as a plucker (was what they called it), plucking dead leaves from the trees, so there I was when the rain started pounding down. To us they issued ponchos of clear plastic before we climbed the ladders to pluck wet leaves with a fingered gripper we triggered at the end of a pole. After a half hour of even that futility they finally called us down and paid us half our contract, for "half of the contract's work," they said. The rain finally died at midnight, and they kept all the girls up late, the beautiful people, to finish off rehearsals and coaching and whatever other whatnot they said.

Thursday broke. The rains began again, draining steadily down. Everything—high school, post office, George's—was closed up for the show. So, there wouldn't have been work, anyway, even if I'd had a job to go to, and I wasn't going to be able to see about finding more work, anyway. So, I wandered out to the main drag about the time the show would be happening, and walked in behind Ted's old hardware store, where a brick propped the back door open. From there rose a flight of stairs to reach the roof, where folding chairs were set out, where a bunch of us locals had already started to gather. We were here because Ted's old hardware store was set away from the action, but mostly because Ted's old hardware store was built with a flat roof. Although the beautiful people hadn't bothered to tent the chairs, so every seat was wet. Instead, everyone bunched the one corner draped over with a tarp. There a table was unfolded to hold a coffee thermos near a bag of paper cups (halfway empty; the thermos was empty all the way). The only other thing on the table was a television that showed the stage, with its speaker hooked up to the sound system cabled to microphones down the street.

Nothing was rolling yet. The beautiful people all milled about, eyeballing their watches and chewing their sandwiches, pointing at the crew and snapping instructions what to do. The girls—in full regalia, blossoming gowns and painted makeup—huddled under tarps jigged up over the staging area. The camera crew and sound crew checked the monitors and cabled connections, sometimes unplugging and replugging a line before taping it back to the ground. I got in a talk with Eduardo, and with Jay and Andy and Yuri, about the chances of catching some cleanup work, even just sweeping and raking and trash. Yuri and Andy had asked about that, but the beautiful people wouldn't commit to hiring, just told them to come back after filming was finished to maybe work something out. Jay looked a little bit hopeful at that (his son was just starting first grade) but Eduardo, who was single like me, gave a look like that sounded like *no*.

The rain was staying, and they hadn't turned on the sound yet, so it was pantomime as the pageant director panned her palm at the rain before ducking back under an awning. She hollered into a headset hooked on her ear, pointing and waving one hand, her other hand pressing the headset tight to her ear. The other beautiful people were shrugging their shoulders, glancing at watches, sitting at mixing boards, or picking at food on a table. We locals were getting antsy, too, especially parents with their daughters in show, saying, "They told us the show would have started by now. Why haven't they started the show?"

Noon passed. Then one o'clock. Right up getting near two, the rain was still dropping—not heavy, but still falling steadily down. The pageant director signaled the camera crew; the cameramen crouched at their cameras, ducking beneath clear plastic sheets that were draped over the tops of the cameras. The extras trotted out from Sara's to press against the sawhorses lining the sidewalks; the pageant director gave the microphone a tap. The sound man at the mixing board thrust a fist out, thumbs up; the pageant director glowed on a smile and stepped out on stage. The extras lining the sawhorses all cheered and waved their arms while a camera hooked to a dolly was towed slowly up the street. "Who's ready for this year's Daughter's Day?" called the pageant director into the microphone, and the extras all waved their arms, shrieking, "We are!"

Among us, up above Ted's, were a few mumbled, "We are's," too. Out now were the camcorders, aimed by parents with daughters in show. At first a few tried to shoot over the parapet, aiming their cameras down the street, but pretty soon they all trained their lenses on the television. From where we listened the echo was terrible—there was a lag between the sound as it squawked from the television and as it boomed from speakers up the street. Little girls sat before the TV, behind them ducked the camcorder parents, and behind them huddled the remainders of us as the daughters were introduced. As every daughter crossed the stage, parents or friends raised fists and cheered. Inez on screen looked a little bit nervous, taut in the glare from the lights. Inez's mother pushed her camera forward, closer to the television, saying, "Look! It's my Inez! There she is!"

(Every time a daughter crossed the stage, the street extras cheered with that terrible echo. After a minute of that, Andy wormed up to the front. He fingered the volume off. Now we could finally understand. The sound was lagged behind the action, but at least we could make out the words.)

Nothing was changed from years ago, from the last Daughter's Day I'd seen. The first part of the show was daughters traipsing to the mic to announce in order: their name, their age, their weight, their interests. Then the daughters changed into swimsuits. They crossed the stage once more, stopping at the mic to tell their goals: *Wedding! Beauty! Children! Peace!* Even in my day these were scripted and had to be memorized ahead of time by the girls. Inez's goals were to travel to South America before graduating medical school, practicing a few years, then having a girl and a boy. "In that order," she said.

(Cue laughter from the extras in the bleachers.)

Normally then would come the first round of judging. But the rain was lapsing then, so they rushed the daughters back into their gowns, herded them back up the street. From there, the beautiful people had them walk the length of the street up to the stage so they could film the opening procession. The cameras followed the daughters, smiling and waving at the crowd of extras who sometimes cheered their names, or whistled and pressed the sawhorses. Halfway through the rain took up, and they had to abort the procession while the daughters stood before heat lamps, drying the raindrops from their gowns. They stood and waited while the sprinkling faded to drizzling, faded to mist, then the beautiful people signaled the daughters to march again. The cameras followed the daughters, smiling and waving at the crowd of extras, who sometimes cheered their names, or whistled and pressed the sawhorses.

Then it was back to their swimsuits and back on stage to start the judging. The judges called not the names of the winners, but the names of the daughters who'd missed the cut. Partway through, Inez was among them. On the roof of Ted's old hardware store, Inez's mother looked crushed, lowered her camcorder. "She didn't even finish the first round."

Talent was what always followed. I knew from my high school days that they cut the first round for talent, so the only daughters left were daughters who could perform something for the cameras. Most of it was music or dancing, making speeches, the usual cycle, but the beautiful people were always looking for something to break the repetition. Lee's youngest daughter Dina did a piece of stunt archery where from twenty paces she could strike a plate spun midair over the stage. Yuri's stepdaughter Michaela had been deep into yoga some years and up on stage twisted her body in strange and balanced contortions to applause from the extras. Trudy (who mostly took care of herself now that her mother was on disability) tried to wheelie her motorcycle across the stage but couldn't quite pull it off. She could do it, too (she'd been an addict now of dirt bikes for years) but her ninety seconds were up, so she had to ramp her motorcycle off the stage. On the TV, the cameras zoomed up to her face to get a good shot of her crying before she let go the clutch and throttled her bike away.

Then it was back to formal gowns for judging another round. The pageant director called names; the daughters called out had to march off the stage. Of the final six, none were daughters I knew (through myself or somebody else) although I recognized one of blondes (I'd seen her with Inez on a couple of occasions). The final round was nothing more than the daughters walking in a circle while the judges looked them over and poked their votes on computer screens. After that, the judges all huddled with the pageant director at their table, where she eyed the votes before stepping back on stage. A drum roll rolled through the speakers, and—from smallest to largest tally—she called out the names of the daughters who weren't going to be named the winner. The last daughter standing was one of the other blondes; she clutched her mouth and broke into tears while the extras whooped and shrieked and whistled to cheer her on. One of the extras ran up to the stage to wrap the blonde in a hug (an extra playing her mother, who was actually on the roof, crying in her circle of friends, "I'm never going to see her, I'm never going to see her, she's going to be a someone," she said). Down on stage, the extra yelled, "I'm so proud you're a winner today, baby!"

In formal gowns, the daughters made the final procession down the street, away from the stage, in toward the outskirts of town. They were followed at last by the winning daughter, waving and cradling roses. The extras cheered her on while she was helped into a limousine. When the limousine turned at the end of the street the pageant director called *cut*. The cheers ended. Then the beautiful people began breaking down the stage. Jay corralled Andy and Yuri and me (and tried to corral Eduardo, too) to talk to the beautiful people about maybe some cleanup work. Eduardo put his hands in his pockets but followed behind us anyway as we walked to the street to try to flag someone who could maybe hire for work. Security was out in force, though, telling us to keep our distance, so in the end we didn't even hear from someone, not even to hear a *no*.

Because Saturday was her mother's regular day off (and she'd taken off Friday, too, according to Inez) the Sunday following was my expectation. Sunday, the swing or the night shift. But Sunday afternoon grayed to evening, blackened to more rain: no moon—no Inez.

That next morning, I drove to the high school. A block away I parked, watched the girls all walk to class. No Inez. Then the bell rang, so I drove to the office. No companies were renting labor, so I drove back home, and again: no Inez. Then Tuesday: back to the high school, back to the office, back to the same old waiting.

Eduardo was seated in the waiting room, waiting for day labor, too. "Hey—you know what a grip is?" he said.

"A grip?"

"Yeah."

"What are you talking about?"

"Like a job, it's like a job, like working with movie cameras and shit. It's one of those jobs you don't think about when you think about making movies."

"A grip?"

"That's what I think it is."

"I don't know. Why do you ask?"

"I never heard of it. Jesse asked me what a grip is. But I didn't know."

"Who's Jesse?"

"Jessica Serra. You know her? Moved here maybe ten years ago, works at the Purina plant. She's got that—what do they call it?—lazy eye."

"I don't know her," I said. That was a half a lie—she was mother to Inez. I pointed at my eye. "I know who you're talking about, though."

"That's what she asked. 'What's a grip?' she said. I didn't know, so that's all I told her."

"Why'd she ask you something random like that?"

"You know last Thursday? She had a daughter in it. Her daughter wasn't the winner, but I guess she ran off with one of the camera crew. A grip. That's why she was asking. Her daughter, she'd run off with this guy, and she doesn't even know the guy's name. All she knows is his job: he's a grip."

"I don't know what that is."

"Yeah, I had to tell her I didn't know what that was, either."

"Run off with one of the camera crew, did she?"

"The daughter? That's what Jesse said. But hey—what can you say? That kind of thing is bound to happen, right?"

"What?"

"You know—the daughters. The girls. They see all the money, the lights, the parade, and the action, and a handful are going to start to think: 'I want a piece of that.'"

"Yeah—I guess. Huh. What can you say?"

Eduardo shrugged. "You can say nothing. Nothing is as much as you can ever say."

If the companies looking to rent day labor don't come looking by afternoon, they never come. So, come two o'clock Eduardo and me split the price of a six pack. Then it was home again, this time driving the main drag of town. The trees were starting to brown and lean and the asphalt was starting to chatter. Yuri, who'd once been a mason, said they used the wrong kind of mix. Or else they poured it too thin, or else both problems together.

Wednesday night was the broadcast of all the different Daughter's Days from the different towns; ours took maybe ten minutes; Inez didn't make the cut. Mostly they just showed the winners, the girls who were driven off in white limousines, escorted to the big cities, where they were promised to be made into someones. Just before getting in the limousines, the different winners from the different towns all wept and promised to the camera that they would never forget their roots. Once she was big and once she was someone, every girl promised she would come home. Once she was big and once she was someone, every girl promised she'd still remember. Those lines were part of the script, probably, although probably that didn't matter. I've yet to hear of daughter who ever managed to bring herself home. You can't place blame—if I was a daughter, if you were a daughter, if anyone was a daughter: it would take some kind of naive to turn back home.

John David Morgan

Rehab Days

Lily left the Psych Ward on the Monday before Easter.

Leaving the Psych Ward was surprisingly simple, starting with signing a small pile of paperwork. She carefully read every word of the first few documents before cautiously committing her Jane Hancock. After that, she quickly reviewed them, and then autographed the final few, after barely scanning them. She wondered if this was real, or some trick, and once she completed the last document, they would tell her she had just agreed to stay another three months. But they let her go, and she soon passed through the now unlocked heavy steel doors. Looking back, she saw the wire-reinforced glass windows of the third-floor wing where she had been sheltered since January. Then she turned into the hallway, then she took the elevator down to the lobby.

She dragged her suitcase along the way. Literally dragging it, since one of the two wheels had locked. She thought this might have been some sort of a test. Maybe, even a final exam. Before her stay, she would have lost her mind and been screaming at a defective wheel. But not now. Now, she quietly continued making her exit, negotiating the uncooperative luggage along, using her right hand. In her left hand, she had a stranglehold on her prescription. It was her passport to the world of the sane.

As soon as the elevator stopped on the first floor, Lily stepped through the open doors, looking for her mother. Her forced smile evaporated, when she realized a few minutes later her mother wasn't there. She walked to the front window, and looked into the parking lot. No, her mother's car wasn't out there. Great. Maybe her mother had gotten tied up, and sent Luke to take her home. Luke was Lily's older brother—older by just a few days short of a year. He was twenty-two, and Lily had just turned twenty-one in the hospital. Luke was so unreliable; she'd probably have to take an UBER home. Lily looked again. Luke's car wasn't there; but . . . wait—was that Luke's girlfriend's car? She turned around and sure enough, there was Luke's girlfriend, asleep on a lobby couch.

Luke's girlfriend was someone he met at Rehab Number Two. She was very, very pretty. She was not very friendly. When Lily first met her last Christmas, she had called her "The Turtle." Sticking her head out of

Luke's room, frowning at Lily, then drawing back in quickly. Or maybe Lily imagined that?

As if on cue, Luke's girlfriend woke up, and saw Lily standing over her. She said a quick hello, or something like it—Lily couldn't quite hear her—then took Lily's bag. She pulled it a few steps, then picked it up and carried it by the side handle to the car. They didn't talk during the drive home. Lily repeated to herself, "I can do this. I can do this. I can do this."

"Home" for Lily and Luke, and now Luke's girlfriend, was their parent's 10,000 square foot house. When Lily and Luke's girlfriend got there, Lily's dog—a Cavalier King Charles Spaniel named Princess—barked her a greeting. Princess was initially excited to see Lily, but then kept running to Luke's girlfriend, then running to the back door and scratching it.

"What's that about?" Lily asked.

"She's become my yapping shadow," Luke's girlfriend said. "It's time for her walk. We've got a regular routine going."

The two of them took Princess for a walk. Since Princess was usually a good judge of character, Lily decided she would give Luke's girlfriend a second chance. Maybe Lily was wrong, she wasn't a turtle. After all, Lily wasn't mentally in a good place last Christmas.

"Oh, yeah," Luke's girlfriend said as they rounded the turn at the end of the cul-de-sac. "Your mom said to tell you she was sorry she couldn't pick you up. She had to meet Luke—he was having some emergency. I don't know what it was. He never tells me anything."

Lily dreaded seeing Luke again. He was constantly giving her advice, especially in front of their parents: one day at a time; fake it till you make it; don't let perfect be the enemy of good; and his favorite: progress, not perfection. Lily had discussed all this in the hospital with her counselor. Why in the world did Luke feel like he could give her advice? Dealing with Luke was something she needed to work on, they decided together.

"I really don't care where he is," Lily said. "Wherever he is, I'm sure he's up to no good."

"I should have known he was up to no good, the minute he asked me to lunch," Lily's mother said to herself.

"Mom—please," Luke said.

Luke and his mother were finishing what had been a pleasant lunch. She was in a hurry to get back to her father in the hospital. It was a little disappointing, but not surprising, that Luke hadn't asked how his grandfather was doing. Luke was a lot like his grandfather, whose liver was now damaged beyond repair. When Luke was at his first rehab, the director of the place had met with the visitors—parents, spouses, pregnant girlfriends, without the addicts, or "clients" as she called them, present—and asked them if there was a history of drug or alcohol abuse in the visitor's families, excluding the client they were there to see. Every hand in the room went up, including hers.

No, Luke didn't ask about his grandfather.

"Luke, I can't keep doing this. You are going to have to learn how to manage your money. How do I know you won't use the money for drugs?"

"It's not for drugs," Luke said. "I didn't want to tell you, but—it's for an abortion."

She didn't actually believe the abortion story, but after several more minutes, she had written him a check, after he promised her, he would go and visit his grandfather in the hospital.

He never did.

She considered telling her husband about Luke asking for the money. But she just couldn't. He was always so busy with his work. The biggest reason, though, was that they were never on the same page when it came to Luke. When she was ready to kick Luke out, he wanted to give him another chance. The night he had driven Luke to the homeless shelter, she had cried her eyes out. She would have gone and gotten him the next day. The director at Luke's first rehab had told them all, the "clients" have to hit rock bottom, before they'll bounce back to a normal life. Someone in the crowd had asked, what happens if they die on their way to rock bottom? The director didn't have an answer for that.

What happened a year later was all her fault, she would tell herself. She should have said "no" to Luke more often.

Easter

Luke and his girlfriend were missing.

Again.

When they finally got home, just like always, they would have a story. A story of where they had been, of why they were held up, of why they couldn't call. No, nothing was wrong. Everything was perfect. Lily actually wished Luke were home, so she wouldn't have to face her aunt alone. It was too soon. She had only been home from the hospital a few days.

She was in her room, dreading Easter dinner. In the hospital, her counselor had talked to her about triggers. Today was a day that was just plain trigger-filled. The first was Easter itself. The first time she had cut herself, as a senior in high school, was on Easter. One of Lily's friends that also cut was a Catholic. It was the whole "Blood of Christ" thing for her, she explained. As a former Presbyterian, and more recently, an agnostic, the "Blood of Christ" meant nothing to Lily. But cutting was one thing she could count on to control her anxiety. It turned out: a razor was the perfect self-medicating tool. Another trigger had been her mother forcing her to wear a dress, which meant she'd have no choice but to shave her legs. Shaving her legs always, always, always, meant cutting. Finally, there was Lily's aunt.

Lily's aunt was her mother's only sibling. She was one of those touchy, feely, hugging, invading personal space people that Lily hated. What made that physical contact unbearable was touching her aunt's leather-like skin, which came from so much time in the sun, laying out at the country club every day of the year except Fourth of July. At least, she had finally given up invading Lily's personal space, since Lily would be so visibly uncomfortable.

Just then, the home intercom in Lily's room crackled. "Lily, dear, please come down to dinner," her mother's voice requested through the speaker.

When Lily entered the dining room, her mother and father, and aunt and uncle, were all seated at the twelve-person table. Her uncle said "hello," while her aunt made a move towards her, caught herself, and also said "hello" before retaking her seat. She had been close enough for Lily to smell the alcohol on her breath, which if she found out, would upset her mother, since there was no drinking ever allowed in the house.

After they all had filled their plates, her aunt said, "Lily, I'm so glad you're back home. They must have had really good food at that hospital. It looks like you've gained quite a bit of weight since I saw you last Thanksgiving."

"I, ah," Lily started, but before she could answer, as the dogs in the living room were barking their heads off, Luke came in through the garage, and joined them in the dining room.

"There's my favorite nephew," Lily's aunt said, embracing Luke in a long hug.

"That's just because I'm your only nephew," Luke said, smiling, sitting down and putting a few bites of food on his plate.

"I'm her only niece," Lily thought. "But she never calls me her favorite niece."

"Luke, how do you stay so thin?" Lily's aunt asked. Something that bothered Lily, besides the reptilian skin, was the way Lily's aunt ate like a bird. Lily considered her to be entirely too thin. Unhealthy, even. She wondered if her aunt was actually, secretly, bulimic.

"I'll bet you're playing a lot of basketball, or maybe jogging." Lily's aunt continued. "You should take Lily with you when you do. She needs to lose several pounds."

Lily was thinking about how Luke had once loved to play basketball. To her knowledge, he hadn't played since the ninth grade, when he got caught with pot at school, and was kicked off the team. Lily could guess why Luke was getting so thin again.

"Lily," her dad said, but she was still in thought.

Maybe she should speak up, and tell her aunt why Luke was always so thin?

"Lily!" her dad said loud enough to get her attention.

"Yes," she said.

"Your uncle is talking to you."

She turned toward her uncle.

"Could you please pass the ham," he said.

Memorial Day

Lily and Luke's girlfriend were taking Princess for a walk on Memorial Day. Several of Lily's neighbors had half-mast American flags mounted to the sides of their houses.

Lily's opinion of Luke's girlfriend had changed. She was not an ugly turtle. She was a beautiful hummingbird, moving so quickly she was just a brightly-colored blur. She wanted to shrink her down, hold her in her cupped hands, and feel her franticly beating heart.

Luke's girlfriend asked Lily, "Are you still cutting?"

Lily asked back, "Are you and Luke still getting high?"

"No."

That was probably a lie, Lily thought, but let it pass.

"I'm not cutting," Lily said.

Which was true. She hadn't cut since Easter. She had told her counselor the truth about that, at their very next weekly session. Lily was actually starting to enjoy her counseling sessions, and staying on her meds, and feeling better.

"What happened before you went to hospital," Luke's girlfriend asked.

Lily had known the question was coming. "Right before I went into the hospital, I was having a tough time in school. I couldn't feel anything. Even after I cut. Nothing, nada."

After a pause. "And?" Luke's girlfriend said.

"And right then and there, I decided. I was not going to let the razor win, that was it."

"That was it?"

"That was it."

"I beat it."

Fourth of July

Lily's father and her uncle were sharing a golf cart at their country club's annual Fourth of July golf scramble. Lily's father approached the first tee and removed the cover from his super-expensive, custom-made driver.

It was a broomstick.

"I can't believe it," Lily's father said.

Lily's uncle laughed out loud. "I've got an extra you can borrow, until you buy a new one at the turn on nine." Then becoming serious. "You need to get Luke into some really good out-of-state rehab, for a really long time."

Lily's father shook his head. His day was ruined. "That would be a great idea, if we could do it. But that's not an option. He's on probation. Can't leave the state. Once they get in the damn system, you're screwed—it really limits your options."

"Are you going to tell your wife about this?" Lily's uncle asked.

"No way," Lily's father answered. "All that would happen, is we would fight about it. She blames me for being so easy on Luke when he was growing up. She says I always had to be the nice guy, a friend. You're his father, she would say, not his damned buddy. And now here we are. You're not going to say anything about it to your wife, are you?"

"Make you a deal," said Lily's uncle. "I won't say anything about the broomstick, and you keep quiet on the beer cart girls."

"Deal," said Lily's father. "What happens in the scramble, stays in the scramble."

When he got home, Lily's father confronted Luke about the missing golf club.

Luke swore that he had pawned it a long time ago. Before. Back when he was using. Well before he had gone to rehab the second time.

"Everything is perfect now," Luke said.

Lily's father never even seriously considered telling his wife what Luke had done. Not with the stress she was under, dealing with her father's illness.

What happened nine months later was all his fault, he would tell himself. He should have played golf more often.

Labor Day

Luke's girlfriend asked him why Lily had been in the psych ward.

"She drove herself crazy being a perfectionist," Luke said. Then he told the story that Lily didn't know he knew, one that he had overheard from his parents.

"It was the semester after we met at rehab. Lily took some special Honors class she didn't even have to have. The teacher told her on day one she didn't believe in giving A's, but Lily took the class anyway."

"What's the big deal about not giving A's?"

"Are you kidding? Lily the perfectionist made straight A's for twelve years of school. She was Valedictorian. She didn't miss a single question on her SAT. And, she had made all A's her first three years of college. Then she got an A minus in that stupid class. The highest grade that teacher had ever given. She started cutting herself, with a thin razor like this,"—here he held his thumb and forefinger an inch and a half apart—"But she just couldn't feel anything that time. She said the razor was dull and stupid."

After a pause, Luke said, "It talked to her."

"Talked to her?" his girlfriend asked.

"It taunted her; it dared her."

"It dared her?"

"It dared her."

"She swallowed it."

Thanksgiving

"Everything looks almost too good to eat," Lily's aunt said to Lily's mom. "Thank you for having us over. I know this makes several years in a row for you, but I promise I'll do it next year."

Lily rolled her eyes, and shook her head. The family was once again seated at the dining room table, "the family" being Lily, her mother and father, and her aunt and uncle.

"Your nephew sends his regrets," Lily's aunt continued. "He would have loved to come, but he's just so busy there at Princeton. And he has the cutest girlfriend now."

It made Lily angry, every time her aunt brought up Lily's cousin going to Princeton. He had only gotten in because Lily's uncle had been an undergraduate, so her cousin was what was called a "legacy." It wasn't even fair. She could have gotten into Princeton, but she had been wait-listed, and ultimately turned down, at her first choice, Yale. But at least she had earned her way into University of Virginia, one of the best non-Ivy schools.

"Well, we should start eating before it gets cold," Lily's father said.

After the food was passed around, Lily's aunt spoke up again.

"He's really doing well at Princeton, at the top of his class now. It won't be long before he'll have to decide which law school to go to. Although his father has his heart set on him going to Harvard Law, like he did."

"Actually," Lily's uncle said, "I'll be happy wherever he goes—that's his decision."

Lily's aunt turned up her nose. It seemed to Lily that she was wobbling in her chair just a bit. Tipsy. She probably had been drinking again before coming to their house.

"I'm just so sorry Luke couldn't be here," Lily's aunt said. "It's just a shame, not being home for Thanksgiving. Where did you say he was?" directing the question to her sister.

"I didn't say," Lily's mother said.

"But it's just so odd that . . . "

Lily interrupted her. "Good God! He's in rehab, okay."

"Rehab?" her startled aunt replied. "On Thanksgiving?"

"Yes, on Thanksgiving," Lily answered. "What the hell. Do you think they just shut down those places, and send everyone home for rehab holidays?"

Lily's mother started to tear up, her lips trembling.

"Lily, mind your manners," her father said.

"But . . . rehab? Isn't this his second time in rehab?" Lily's aunt said.

"Actually," Lily calmly replied. "This is his third time. The second time was the Saturday Surprise."

"The Saturday what?" Lily's aunt said, desperately looking around the table, but no one was coming to her rescue.

"The Saturday Surprise," Lily said. "It was last year, when dad finally checked his bank account, and saw how many thousands of dollars Luke had written in checks to himself. Dad said that was it, and he drove Luke to the homeless shelter downtown and dropped him off. It was a Friday night."

"Oh, my," her aunt said.

"Then the next morning, Dad yelled at me to check my bank account. But I never set up online banking, so he was all mad, and had to drive me to the bank. And we were at a stoplight, when the car started shaking, like an earthquake or something. Then Luke popped up from the back of the SUV, where the third-row seats were down."

"Popped up?"

"Yes. He had walked all the way from downtown—twenty miles— and broke into our garage and slept a few hours in the back of Dad's car. And after that, he begged Mom and Dad to pay for his second rehab."

"Second rehab?"

"Yes, second rehab. Like I said, last year. Then last month, he got stopped by the police. They arrested him on possession of heroin, and drug paraphernalia—he had lots of needles in his car. So now, he's back in rehab, this time for six months. He says it's a lot better than jail."

"I suppose rehab would be . . . better than jail?" Lily's aunt uncertainly said.

"Yep. There you go, you're all caught up."

Lily then addressed her uncle.

"Could you pass the turkey, please?"

Christmas

Lily was so happy! Luke's girlfriend was actually going to play video games with her in her room. Lily told her father's joke; they were playing on the most expensive video game system in America, since it had been bought back from being pawned by Luke at least a dozen times.

After they had played a while, Luke's girlfriend said, "I really miss Luke. Six months in rehab is a long time, and he's only half-way done."

Lily had been thinking about saying something for a while, and decided now was the time.

"The best thing you could do, is get away from Luke," she said.

Luke's girlfriend had a hurt look, but didn't answer.

"Luke has issues. Real issues," Lily continued. "I'm not sure he's not some kind of sociopath. He doesn't care about anyone but himself."

"I'll tell you the truth," Luke's girlfriend said. "I honestly have had those same thoughts. But I just don't agree with that now. He can be such a great person; he's so smart, and he's sweet, and funny, but then other times." She shook her head. "After we got out of rehab, I wanted to stay clean—I did stay clean—but Luke just couldn't. Or wouldn't. I lied to you before—I was doing drugs with Luke before he got caught."

"I thought so," Lily said. "What about now?"

"Now I'm not. You remember I was sick for a week after Luke got arrested? That's when I stopped. I feel so much better now. Almost like a normal person."

"What will you do when Luke gets out?" Lily said.

"I honestly don't know. Luke has talked about doing it one more time, then both of us quitting forever. I *really* miss him," she said and started to cry.

Lily reached out and gave Luke's girlfriend a hug. Luke's girlfriend pulled her closer, then closer still. She let Lily loose, just enough to face her. Then she kissed Lily. Before Lily knew what was happening, they were on Lily's bed together.

Lily considered herself mono-sexual. She had never been with a male, or a female. What happened next was something she wasn't prepared for. She cried when it was over. It would be the only time it happened.

A week after the video game evening, Lily discovered she was missing the five hundred dollars she had kept not very well hidden in her room.

She asked Luke's girlfriend about the money. She swore she hadn't touched it. Was Lily sure she hadn't just misplaced it? After Lily thought about it, she hadn't checked on the money since before Luke went back to rehab. He may have stolen it. Or maybe it was his girlfriend, and she had seduced Lily to cover her tracks, knowing Lily wouldn't dare tell her parents?

What happened three months later was all her fault, she would tell herself. Luke's girlfriend may have used her money to buy the drugs the day Luke got out of rehab. Regardless, she should have told someone about Luke wanting to get high one last time. It was all her fault.

Easter, again (otherwise known as "later")

Lily's counselor congratulated her on one year out of the psych ward—although not in those exact words. There had been a few ups and downs, but generally, things were going well.

Until Good Friday.

Lily's maternal grandfather died finally on Good Friday.

Although she'd been preparing herself for this day in recent sessions with her counselor, it still stung when her mother yelled at her. "Your grandfather's funeral will be next Friday, when Luke gets home. You will wear a dress. And yes, you will shave those hairy legs."

Later that night, Lily was in her oversized whirlpool tub, shaving her hairy legs.

She accidentally nicked herself.

The blood rushed out, excited to see her again. It had been such a long time!

She immediately put pressure on the cut with a wash cloth. Then she finished shaving without incident.

When she was finished, she calmly put the razor down on the wide ledge of the tub.

Even if the razor had been screaming at her, she couldn't possibly have heard it.

Not over the sound of her own voice.

"Progress, not perfection. Progress, not perfection. Progress, not perfection."

Luke left Rehab Number Three on the Thursday after Easter.

His girlfriend picked him up.

They shot something new in the parking lot: heroin laced with fentanyl.

One of them died.

Julie Beals

Joint Attention

When we'd been married for six months, Carter and I began playing tennis at the Albuquerque Sportsplex. It was adjacent to a miniature golf course, and when we were out on the court, dashing back and forth with rackets in hand, we could see a pastel-colored windmill making slow rotations in the distance. Part of the agreement, when we started playing tennis, was that we weren't actually going to play. We weren't going to compete. We'd only rally, and, to make it fun—or at least, to give ourselves an objective—we'd try to rally for twenty-five consecutive hits. Twenty-five hits in which neither of us missed the ball.

It was Carter's idea. "I don't want us opposing each other," he'd intonated, a hand on my shoulder. "If we're going to take precious time out of our schedules to do an activity, I want it to unite us. I want us to be on the same team."

And I liked this, when he initially proposed it. It struck me as romantic. Him, stamping down a stake of solidarity in the arid, ungiving soil. Driving it in with his heel. A guarantee that, should we ever end up apart, it probably wouldn't be the result of a decision *he'd* made.

So, we rallied to twenty-five. And we rallied to twenty-five. We gulped water from a recycled *V8* jug, passing it back and forth between us. I cast aside layers when the game became more vigorous. Carter used the front of his T-shirt to wipe his forehead. We were in complete unison; there wasn't so much as a droplet of tension on our court. We'd found the kind of marital simplicity that might have piqued me a bit, had it not been mine. But it was mine. And then, when I started consistently missing the twenty-fifth shot, it wasn't anymore.

I want to clarify something before I go any further: Carter is not a bad guy. It's just that, without meaning to, he made our home into a place that was uninhabitable for me.

I always knew he preferred quiet over noise. I'll admit—I even knew before we started dating. I remember driving across the Great Plains with him, back when we were in our "undefined" stage—somewhere between lovers and weary friends—and noticing that he didn't want to turn on the radio. Or philosophize, or vacantly chat. Or sigh in anticipation of the next gas station. He was even reluctant to crack open the windows, for the *whirring* sound they'd make. We traversed the Great Plains in total silence. Nothing but visual input, and an unlimited amount of it. Golden yellow in the bottom half of our visual field; delectable blue in the top. I thought that was romantic, too.

So, it's partially my fault. Isn't it? I knew who he was; I knew his attributes. The night he proposed marriage, straddling me, his knees cornered on each of my hips, he implored: "Please only agree to this if it's actually what you want." He kept his face a good two feet from mine. I was fastened down, yes—I was secured—but I wasn't pinned. I knew I had the option of saying no.

Let's talk about the sounds that I was hearing day in and day out. The *pock* of a tennis racket making contact with a rubbery ball, right in the center of the strings. That sweet spot. And the occasional dissonant *pock*, a duller sound, when the ball would hit the rim. The fricative sweep of our front door as we lumbered into the house, keys in hand. The insulation strip brushing against our welcome mat. The unoiled creak of faucet handles; the sound of water splattering in the sink. And then, of course: Carter's very occasional comment. Comments which were always piercing, pleasing, and like nourishment to me. The way, after eleven hours together and zero utterances, he'd materialize behind me with a hand warm on my neck: "The power's out on the entire east side of Albuquerque. I was thinking we should check on Annie and Lathan." (A couple who runs a private rehab center on the east side.)

See? Good guy.

But then there were the sounds I wasn't hearing. Carter had essentially banned—or successfully negotiated, depending on your terminology—all noise-generating devices. This included microwaves and washing machines with audible beeps. We'd purchased a specialty microwave, intended for the hearing-impaired, which emitted a flashing blue light in lieu of beeping. And no vacuum cleaners. No dachshund, which would have been my pet of choice, because no barking, and no yipping to spring up on furniture or garner an extra snack. Fans were to remain off. The click of an overhead fan, its chain swaying, was known to render Carter berserk. I once watched, mesmerized, as he developed an eye twitch in response to a particularly gesticulative woman seated next to him at a benefit dinner. She wore a charm bracelet.

You have to admit: It's fascinating in the abstract. A man with such hypersensitivity, he had to reduce input as if allergic. As if too much exposure would be fatal. But you can't live in the abstract. You've got a pulse and fleshy body, and a nervous system and an appetite. And I guarantee you, your heartbeat will quicken when you're frightened. And I guarantee you, you'll grieve, and yearn, and eventually go septic when you don't get something you legitimately need.

One day, I undressed to take a shower. I turned the faucet handle, engendering that familiar *creak*. A treasured sound after a day of silence. The hot water flowed forth, and a billowing steam began to roll over our bathroom fixtures, like a mist over mountaintops. I stepped into the tub, one foot after the other, as the bathroom transformed into something akin to an outdoor environment. There was the scent of the strawberry shampoo. The feeling of lather encasing my skull, withdrawing oil from the thoroughfares of my scalp. The lather sliding down my body, riding the curves of my back and exiting off my heels, assimilating itself into the pooling outwash.

Whenever I took a shower, I cued myself to pay attention to all the sounds. The water as it blasted from the showerhead and splatted against the tub. My conditioner bottle, hiccupping as I squeezed it. I'd even rotate my head sometimes, and angle an ear directly up at the showerhead, allowing water to fill my outer ear canal. This produced a low rumbling, as though water was boiling somewhere, deep in a well—and when my ear canal was full, it produced the generalized muted sound of being underwater in a swimming pool.

Here's why I'm telling you this: I was lost in the euphoria of the shower, when suddenly all of the sound cut out, and then all the light in the bathroom was abruptly gone, and I felt my knees become light-headed, weightless.

I found myself, later, crouching in the tub. The water was still blasting over me. One of my legs was fully extended, and my arms were draped haphazardly over my body, as if I'd been asleep and somehow stretching at the same time. The back of my head was sore in a concentrated spot. I stood up, steadied myself against the shower wall, and wrapped a towel around my torso.

I left the bathroom to find Carter. I began rehearsing my story: *Strangest thing. I think I fell in the shower. I don't know how.* But from the moment I opened the bathroom door, I noticed that our house was altered. The hallway was different—broader. The floor was carpeted. The walls were covered in an emerald green wallpaper, patterned with gold palm trees. Not our wallpaper. We hadn't even installed wallpaper.

My breath halted. How had I ended up in someone else's house? Or had I been in someone else's house when I started my shower, and just wasn't remembering? Whose house was this? Had I hit my head so hard I had brain damage? I felt a flush of panic encroach across my cheeks.

I located the staircase and descended stairs one at a time, feeling like an intruder in someone's private residence. It even occurred to me that, once sighted, one of the family members that lived here might call the cops on me. I had thought I'd been on the second floor, where *our* bathroom was located in *our* house, but swiftly realized that I'd been on the third floor. Carter and I didn't have a third floor. I passed a bamboo plant in the hallway; its branches snagged on my towel and bounced backwards as I stepped around it. I saw a University of Wisconsin T-shirt that had been ironed and pressed into a picture frame. Not ours. And I began to hear voices from what I assumed was the first floor. More than one voice.

After a pause that lasted several minutes, I presented myself at the bottom of the stairs. I figured that, at the very least, I would soon clear up the mystery of where I was and what had happened.

I expected shock. Dumbfounded expressions, cautioned tones. But that's not what I found at all. I was met with expressions I knew—those belonging to my roommates from five years prior, back when Carter and I were just beginning to date, just beginning to lace our fingers together during car rides to the farmer's market. Talon, Anna, and Flor.

"Why are you in a towel?" Flor queried, laughing radiantly from where she sat, playing Blackjack.

How to explain, how to explain. I don't know how long I was in that house—how long I was in the past—but I eventually woke up in my present-day bathtub. My head was still sore in one spot. The water was still blasting over me, my skin red and prickled with heat. But I was definitely in the right house. I found Carter in our kitchen, silently grating a bulb of ginger. I saw the back of his head; a haircut I'd given him with an electric clipper. I said nothing.

I saw a doctor.

"This is often how seizures present," said my PCP. "For instance, in a grand mal seizure, it's common for a person to collapse and lose consciousness for the full duration of the episode. And, yes, it's sometimes the case that the person won't remember having collapsed."

But if I had epilepsy, wouldn't I have known about it? I was in my 30s, at this point. Wouldn't I have had other seizures in the past?

"It *is* possible that you've had other seizures," my PCP answered with a tone of finality, as if her statement carried with it an encyclopedia of associated information and could stand on its own. After an impregnated pause, during which I could feel her eyes scanning over my person, she added: "Not all seizures cause a person to collapse and experience muscle spasms. There are some types that appear much more subtle from a third-party perspective. And not all seizures are caused by epilepsy."

She told me they would conduct an EEG—hook me up to a machine and look at my brain waves, to screen for epilepsy. We scheduled it for a date two weeks from then.

"Were you looking at any bright lights before you collapsed?" she asked.

No.

"No flashing lights?"

No.

"Were there any loud sounds? Loud music, hammering?"

I grinned limply.

When Carter and I played tennis that weekend—just three days after the alleged seizure I never told him about—I began a trend that I would continue, in agony, for several months.

He volleyed to me. *Hit.*

I volleyed back to him. *Hit.*

He volleyed to me. *Hit.*

Nineteen hits. And then twenty, twenty-one, twenty-two, twenty-three, twenty-four—and inexplicably, a *whoosh.* Air whizzing through the strings of my racket. Nothing. I'd missed the ball.

Carter wasn't at all perturbed, the first time. We tried again to volley to twenty-five, but even when we arranged the game such that the twenty-fifth shot would land on him, I'd miss the twenty-fourth and we'd have to start all over again.

I remember trekking back to the car afterward, a nylon hoodie bunched under my armpit and Carter swinging our *V8* jug back and forth at his side. He lifted the back of his hand to my forehead, as if checking for a fever, and then smiled at me—wryly, lovingly—as if to say: *Just kidding, just kidding.*

In the days that followed, I took several unextraordinary showers. I shifted from place to place within our home, as if waiting for something to jump out at me—something to leap forward, seize me by the shoulders, and rattle me as it extolled the sublimity of what I'd experienced. *What are you doing? You should be phoning National Geographic! They should be helicoptering you to Harvard Medical School! You should be studied. You broke the space-time continuum by way of an epileptic fit!*

I was noticing, too, that the soundlessness of our home was becoming more difficult to ignore. I suppose I'd initially adapted to it. From the time that Carter and I first started dating, I began wading into an acclimation with silence, and I slipped deeper and deeper in, my clothes becoming weightless and undulating about me, as the years progressed. But now, it was as if I'd drawn my legs up out of that acclimation and was now sitting at its border, holding my knees to my chest and shivering.

"It is *quiet* here," I texted to my sister.

One afternoon I returned from reading a magazine on our back porch. I cherished the *squeak* the door made as it rubbed against our hardwood floor. So unashamed, unselfconscious. *It could make a sound if it wanted to make a sound,* I thought. It had been a particularly low day for me; a particularly soundless day. I saw Carter sitting cross-legged on our chaise with a legal pad in his lap, and I knew, without needing to ask, that he didn't want to be interrupted. *The soundlessness in here!* As I drifted across the living room, I passed the hutch where Carter and I store miscellanea. In its center is a wide and shallow drawer. I knew that I'd stashed a pair of headphones inside it, long ago.

I took a lazy step backwards and paused at the hutch. The height of my shoulder was such that my hand hung level with the drawer. My knuckles were practically brushing up against its knob. The length of a pause before a kiss.

Dare I?

I did dare. I collected the headphones into the private capsule of my hands and retired to our bedroom, leaving Carter behind with his legal pad. I lay on our bed, plugged the headphones into my phone, and let my eyelids fall shut. Chopin first; then The Raincoats; then Stevie Wonder. Oh, the things I'd forgotten. It had been years since I'd listened to music, giving it my full attention. We never turned the radio on when we were in the car. We didn't own a radio at home. Our laptops and cell phones were perennially on mute. Oh, the glory of a private concert in your ear canals. I'd forgotten one could do that; one could enjoy high decibels of sound, solely in their own ears.

This went on, like a vacation from reality—like a new, enticing aspect of reality—until Carter noticed that I'd been wearing headphones for a week.

Over a dinner of stuffed peppers, he chose to communicate: "It makes me feel like you don't want to be around me. Like you're wishing you were somewhere else."

That night, the headphones were returned to the hutch. When I later escaped to the bathroom, to take a shower and gasp, teary-eyed, I had another seizure.

When I woke up in the bathroom of my past, Flor was waiting outside the door with a pack of Stella Artois and a beach towel, rolled like a burrito.

She surveyed me, a puzzled expression through her bangs. "I thought you said a fifteen-minute shower! I was worried, I almost broke the door down on you."

Apparently, in this day from my past, Flor and I had planned to participate in our signature ritual: Venturing to the woods that lined the back of our house—which we weren't *entirely* sure lay within the bounds of our property—and lighting a fire in the pit we'd built. We'd do this in the daytime. We'd pretend we were in a trendier state—Massachusetts, Pennsylvania—and already ensconced in jobs that deeply satisfied us and relationships with guys who understood us. We drank a lot of beer down there.

The alcove surrounding the pit was like a lava lamp in its quality of light. A kaleidoscope of greenery. The trees enclosing it—silver maples, southern red oaks—formed a canopy that was nearly spherical. Whenever Flor and I were near it, I got the sensation that we were trespassing on sacred ground. Something that should have been recognized by the national park service, commemorated with signage. A stop for tourists.

"Have you and Carter talked about marriage?" Flor asked, when we were situated, shoulder to shoulder, on the beach towel.

How to answer that? I wondered if Flor and I had held this exact conversation in my past. I didn't remember it, but surely I'd forgotten the great majority of my conversations from years past. I wondered what my former self had said, if this was indeed a question that Flor had actually posed five years ago.

"I think it has come up once or twice," I said, brushing my bangs off my forehead, which were as wet as if they'd been spritzed. "But no definitive position at the moment."

Later, when it was blackout dark and we were trudging back to the house, high-stepping through overgrown grass, Flor said: "I can't wait to be in the next stage of my life. Have my own house, start creating a family of my own. Don't get me wrong—I love living here, with you guys—but I also feel ready to be in that next stage."

I remember thinking, as we opened the back door and yellowish light from the interior of the house flooded over us, that she was deluded. This stage, right where we were at that very moment, was something to be treasured. This stage had an aura of comfort that was not present in that next stage. Or at least, it hadn't been for me. When we presented at the living room, Talon and Anna were sprawled out with their socks on the coffee table. They turned to us, animating in expressions of joy that reminded me of the bouncing, skittered dance a dachshund performs when its owner comes home. "You're *back*!" they cried, nearly in unison. "We were waiting, we wanted to see if you'd play Blackjack."

Popcorn crackled in the microwave. Someone was playing The Strokes from their laptop—"Ask Me Anything." I recognized the song. Four-way conversation erupted between my roommates, punctuated by guffaws.

When the popcorn was done, the microwave beeped twice, loudly.

Back on the tennis court again, approaching the twenty-fifth hit.
Carter volleyed to me. *Hit.*
I volleyed to him. *Hit.*

Then he volleyed to me on what should have been the twenty-fifth hit, the grand finale, the singular motion that would end the game and send us strolling back to the car, content—when, *whoosh*. Air splicing through the strings. Nothing at all. I'd missed the ball by what must have been a full foot. When I whirled around to see where it went, its trajectory was far from where I'd planted myself.

By this point, Carter had picked up on the pattern. I never missed any other shots. Also, we weren't playing competitively; we were practically bunting the ball to one another, intentionally serving up shots the other could hit. Over and over, I only missed the last one.

Carter had a hand on his waist. He was crushing a small rock against the court with the tip of his racket. He didn't look at me.

"Do you wanna just go home?" I asked, tentatively, after retrieving the ball. I was panting. "I mean, we made it to twenty-four. That's pretty good!"

He didn't say anything. He was still looking at the rock instead of me.

I experimented with a deliberate laugh. "Maybe we should just adjust our goal to twenty-four hits. I mean, in the long-run, it's hardly any different."

Carter nodded, looking pensive, and then turned and ambled over to our *V8* jug.

No headphones to stream a private concert. No overhead fan. No beeping from the washing machine to tell me our sheets are ready for the dryer. No dachshund with shining eyes, whimpering. No windchimes on the porch. No charm bracelets. Carter—in silence—hunched over a spread of manila folders, work he'd toted home on Friday.

Dying. Dying.

I took a shower in the late afternoon, even though I'd already taken one that morning, after the Sportsplex. I turned the water as hot as it would go. The steam inched across the room and thickened. I rubbed strawberry shampoo in my hair in a circular motion, operating on autopilot, thinking: *Just relax. Enjoy this. Enjoy it. Relax. Keep your limbs loose. Get ready for your knees to give way. Just let it happen. It doesn't have to hurt. Come on; relax.*

I couldn't induce it. I squeezed my eyes tight, trying to force one facet of a seizure. I even tried holding my breath. Could lightheadedness induce a seizure? I sobbed under the showerhead. I knew the water would mask the sound.

Back on the tennis court, Carter was the one to start the volley. That way, the twenty-fifth shot would be his. But he never got to make it because I swung and missed the twenty-fourth. I could hear the ball bouncing—*pock, pock, pock*—behind me, away from the spot where my sneakers were planted. The sun was baking us, scouring our skin like disinfectant. I was reminded, in that moment, that sunlight, too, is considered an element. Standing there in my sports bra and shorts, with no sunglasses or visor, I was at the mercy of the elements.

I was also at the mercy of my husband.

Carter swooped his racket through the air, pissed, in a way I'd never seen before. It reminded me vaguely of something of something that professional tennis players do, on television. But he didn't say anything until I was reaching for the hoodie that I'd flung to the side of the court.

"I guess I should have asked a long time ago, but why are you doing this?"

I stood parallel to him, still breathing hard. Rightly convicted, but at the same time, very much not.

When I didn't answer, he tried again: "Is this some kind of passive aggressive swipe at me? Is that what this is?"

I vowed that it was all happening by accident. That I truly wasn't trying to mess up the game. I always tried to hit that last shot; I always fully intended to. I wasn't sure what was happening.

"Bullshit," was Carter's answer. "You're forgetting, I've played opposite you for a year now. I know how you play. And I know you. You're not even trying to hit that last shot. It's insane; you miss it by a full foot."

I denied it, beseeching him.

"What are you so upset about?" he yelled. It was the loudest vocal projection I've ever heard him produce. "Just tell me!" He slung the *V8* jug he'd been drinking from back onto the court, in a motion that was about 40% more forceful than it needed to be. It bounced twice, then rolled away. "Just tell me so we can fuckin' hash it out, and you can stop trying to subliminally send me a message over a fuckin' tennis match."

Two f-bombs. A record.

In this moment, I have to admit—a part of me was nearly turned on. I was experiencing a mercurial, hyper-speed sort of delight within the thermometer-like frame of my upright body. This was the most my husband had said to me since the first day we met. The most abundant, free-flowing speech he'd ever gifted. All the words rolling off his tongue, all the intent, the intellect. I was aroused by it. But the other parts of me were recoiling. I was terrified of his next blow, be it verbal or demonstrative.

Carter retrieved the *V8* jug, snatched up the car keys, and began a purposeful trudge back to our car. His arm flew up behind him, in my direction, as if to say: *Done with this. Done with you.*

I heard my voice catapulting after him, high-pitched and breaking. "Wait! Hold on! Don't just walk off!"

But all I could see was the back of his head. The haircut I'd so scrupulously given him, my fingers scissoring through his hair, my knuckles brushing against the skin of his neck.

Hold on, I said again. But this time only loud enough for me to hear.

That night, I careened into seizure-land. One minute I was squeezing the conditioner bottle—miserable, throbbing—and then I was buckling into darkness, all sound fading out. The last thing I heard was the conditioner bottle knocking against the floor of the tub.

In the world of five years ago, I sat on the wooden steps of the back porch, texting Flor. The woods that lined our backyard were in sight. Fireflies pulsed on and off around its undergrowth.

My text: *Really upset. Hard to explain. Are you around?*

Flor texted me back, emphatically. She wasn't home but promised she would be in ten minutes. She'd find me.

I waited for her. I tried to let the sights and sounds of nature pacify me—the sky transmuting into a ruthless violet, the cicadas reminding the whole living world of their presence. The back porch light blinked on, automatically. I wasn't wearing a sweatshirt. Goosebumps rose on my arms.

Eventually, Anna, not Flor, came out on the porch and settled down beside me.

"It's *frosty* out here," she canted. Anna rubbed the fluted arms of her sweater one by one. She observed my face, my posture—the cell phone that lay in the center of my lap, where my last text to Flor hung, unanswered. "Waiting for an epiphany?"

"She never showed," I said, lifting my phone.

"Who?"

"Flor."

"Ah." Anna embarked on a slow nod. "She was supposed to meet you out here?"

"Yeah."

"I hate to ask, but did you hint that you were upset?"

I turned toward Anna, lasering her with scrutiny. "What's that supposed to mean?"

I remembered that Flor and I had been close, back when we lived in this house. I remembered that we'd been legitimate friends, not just roommates. The raucous belly-laughter, the beer, our musings out by the firepit. I knew we'd shared our deepest thoughts and feelings. But that's all I could remember.

"Flor is one of those people who feels whatever the people around her are feeling. Super empathetic, you know? So, you can imagine that if she's not in the mood for a downswing—and she's usually not—she's probably not gonna leap at the opportunity to converse with someone who's experiencing one."

Her words made a *thud* in my chest. Flor didn't show up, intentionally? She intentionally didn't show up? I studied the dark, willing the fireflies to reappear at the line of the woods. But they didn't.

Anna rested a hand on my shoulder. "You can try talking to her about it. Maybe she won't do this next time. Or you can not talk to her about it, let this go, and just concentrate on the qualities of hers that you *do* like." Anna squeezed my shoulder and stood up.

I woke in the house that Carter and I had purchased together. The present time. I turned off the showerhead, wrapped a towel around my torso, and went looking for him. My face was flushed from the hot water. If I hadn't been continually lifting the corner of my towel to my face, I might not have even realized that I was crying.

Downstairs, there was no sight of him. On the whiteboard that lives by our fridge, I saw a message in marker: *Went to get gas. Be back soon.* And beneath those two fragments, Carter's signature sign-off: Love—. The word "love," with an em dash extending it. Sometimes the em dash was shorter, like a minus sign, and other times it was longer, as if he'd intended to draw an arrow but gave up at the shaft.

I situated myself at the bay window that overlooks our driveway. I felt like a dachshund, waiting for their someone to come home. On the floor beside me was an archive box that we'd been intending to put in storage. It hadn't been taped up. A bundle of old, textured curtains was packed at the top, alongside a pair of 10 lb. weights and stack of glossy photographs. I picked up the photographs. I thumbed through them slowly, appreciating the subdued *shhh* they made as they slid beneath one another.

Shhhhh. I lifted my towel again and pressed it to my face.

In one photograph, Carter and I were stopped beside our car during our trip across the Great Plains. There were other travelers around us. People had pulled to the side of the road and were pointing their cameras at an expanse of gold, where, 50 or 60 yards away, a gigantic bison was grazing. It was close enough that we could sense the texture of its wooly down. The power stored in its musculature.

But that wasn't the focus of the photograph. Carter and I had handed our camera to an amiable passerby, because, somehow, out in the middle of absolutely nowhere, miles upon miles of wheat, we'd managed to drive over a tomahawk. It was the size of a hammer, and its blade had hacked into one of our back tires at a nearly perfect 45-degree angle. It hung from the tire's side, an unwanted souvenir. Red and teal beads dangled from its neck on leather strings.

In the photograph, everyone was turned toward the bison. Everyone except Carter and me. Both of us were crouching in the gravel beside our car, hilarity reverberating in our faces, jointly marveling at the cause of our flat tire.

Samina Hadi-Tabassum

Khalid

On August 24, to celebrate the end of the warm summer months, Khalid threw a party that evening for a hundred families in Lahore. The guests arrived at eight o'clock sharp as indicated on the invitation. The night was soft and warm. The jasmine flowers were blooming in the garden. Strings of tiny yellow lights hung down from the walls and balconies of Khalid's white stucco mansion. Around ten o'clock at night, after eating plates of Sindhi biryani, Punjabi samosas and gulab jamun for dessert, men and women dressed in silk sarees and sherwanis slowly streamed out of the house and gathered under the red Bedouin tent pitched in the back garden, away from the public streets in the front of the house. The women gathered at the rear of the tent and the men gathered near the front of the tent.

The children were still running around in the dark, chasing fireflies and climbing the small pomegranate trees with their bare feet, wobbling the red globes of fruit while hanging upside down from the branches. The young girls had lost their duppatas throughout the night and now these colorful duppatas were scattered across the green grass like neon serpents; there were wrinkles stretched across the boys' kurtas and pajamas. The children's shoes were piled into one corner of the garden as they ran around barefoot. None of the teenage girls and boys were allowed to come to the party, only young children under ten years of age. The teenagers were told to stay home that night and that the party was not for them. The servants in their respective homes stood outside the doors of the young women so no one could enter into their bedrooms at night after the older adults returned to their assigned homes.

The last time the guests came to a party like this was at the start of the monsoon season and the party went deep into the night. The children were told to sleep inside the carpeted hallways while their mothers waited to take them home, well past their bedtime. In some parties across Lahore, the whole event went on until the early morning hours and chai had to be served for the guests to stay awake until their numbers were called. But here at Khalid's party the whole event took no more than a few hours and the guests knew they would head back inside their homes around midnight. Still, the children were restless and tired and kept coming over to their mothers and begging to go home, tugging at their arms and legs. "Mummy, mummy, let's go," they wailed as they looked up into their mothers' worried eyes and tired faces, their makeup now slightly smeared and their pressed hair disheveled.

Soon the men gathered near the microphone at the front of the podium. They were talking about the recent election, cricket matches, and their children's schools. They smiled and laughed among themselves in their huddle but gave furtive glances at the women clad in bright embroidered clothes, adorned in layers of gold jewelry—their glass bangles chiming rhythmically like nightingales. The women gossiped about each other, their mothers-in-law, and the latest soap opera serial. After fifteen minutes under the tent, Khalid checked his watch and then passed a giant glass bowl around the tent toward the women's side. Each woman took out her house keys from her purse and placed them in the bowl. The women prepared themselves to call out their children's names and gather them around the folds of their silk clothes. The children did not always come when their names were called but the women knew that they could not ask their husbands to find their young children. The children had to go home with their mothers. Some of the women stayed in the tent waiting for their children to come to them while others gathered the children from the house, garden, and hallways to come out to the tent. The infants were held in their arms and rocked to sleep as they waited for the men to get into the queue and begin. Ishaan came running to his mother standing under the tent, carrying his sandals in his hands. His mother chided Ishaan for not bringing his younger brother along and made him go back and find Shezaan in the shadows of the night garden.

Khalid made his way to the podium to begin the event. He was a tall, handsome man with a full beard and broad shoulders. He wore a white sherwani with a red rose in its front pocket and an embroidered kufi hat that was woven with gold thread. His wife Zara was also a beautiful woman dressed in a red silk saree. They only had one child and people surmised that Zara wanted to remain youthful for her husband. By the time Khalid finished testing the microphone at the podium, someone passed the glass bowl of keys to Khalid and the tent grew silent. A soft murmur began to spread across the tent. "We're starting on Pakistani time tonight folks," Khalid joked. "We would have been done by now if we were in America." Khalid's brother-in-law Farhad came up quickly and placed the heavy, three-panel wooden chilman next to the podium along with two other servants. The male guests were hesitant to help

Farhad and instead stepped back a few feet from the panel. It was a beautiful sandalwood panel with different-facing intricate peacocks etched into each panel. The women will have to walk up to the panel with their young children and stand behind it, waiting patiently for the man who would take them home that night, the man with her keys in his hand. No one would see them walking together to their cars behind the large wooden panel.

Farhad stood back from the panel and held the glass bowl, stirring the mound of keys inside, while Khalid spoke into the microphone. Khalid often used a large wooden box instead of the glass bowl so no one could see the keys inside, but he could not find the wooden box tonight. One of the servants must have moved it from behind his bedroom armoire but he was too embarrassed to ask them to find it. At the last moment, Zara decided to use the glass bowl where they stacked their fresh fruit at the kitchen table. Mangoes, bananas and pomegranate often rose in a cascade of colors from the glass bowl. "Well, ladies and gentlemen, you can see how the wooden box we used for years is not here tonight. I must have misplaced it, so Begum Zara was able to quickly use her clever mind to find us a solution for tonight. Perhaps the wooden box will be found the next time we have a party, although it looked quite battered and maybe needs to retire just like me!" chuckled Khalid into the microphone.

Khalid now motioned his only child, Daniyal, to come and hold the glass bowl still on the stool next to the podium. Daniyal held his eleven-year old hands tightly along the top of the bowl while his father moved his fingers around shaking the mound of keys up and down. Over the years, the mound of keys kept growing as more and more families heard about the parties Khalid throws. A few weeks ago, Khalid wrote out invitations to all the families in the compound he wanted to invite and asked them to label their keys with their house numbers. Every woman was asked to tie a string around the metal ring and carefully label only the numbers onto a chit of cardboard paper. Of course, Khalid spent a lot of time thinking of which families to invite. They had to be open minded and not religious. No one with ties to the Pakistani military and no one with ties to any masjid and madrassa. They had to be well educated families who had lived abroad and preferred Western clothes, music, and lifestyles. They often tended to be the families who built swimming pools once they moved into the compound and made sure the concrete walls covered the wives in their swimsuits. The men also had to drink, preferably whisky and brandy. Khalid made sure to offer each man at the party at least a few drinks before they made their way to the tent. Khalid also met with each man at their home before he dropped off the invitation in their hands, greeting their wives, and memorizing the ages of the children. Some said that Khalid made you recite his favorite Urdu poems before joining him at his house and others thought he made the men flog themselves in the back rooms of his house as if they were Shias in Muharram. But none of this was true. Khalid knew when he looked the man in the eyes whether this man was a lover of women, a lover of flesh, and all the tenderness that comes with it and without the guilt of sin in their hearts—a man he could trust.

Sometimes the families Khalid invited left before the party made its way to the tent, not having the nerves to go through with the exchange at the end, leaving an uneven number, and Khalid and Zara having to step out of the queue. Khalid was no longer angry at families for leaving. He knew they were living in different times now in Pakistan where religion was all around them. What happened behind closed doors a decade ago was no longer tolerated. There were many times when Khalid thought that they would get caught and taken away to jail, both he and Zara. They made sure to never disclose the names of the guests and asked everyone to tear up the invitations after receiving them by hand. Khalid was very good at being discreet and nobody in the government suspected him of wrongdoing in his silk sherwani, parked Mercedes and a security guard at the gate. Khalid was much more hushed than ever before under the Nawaz Sharif regime, but he made sure there was an inheritance set aside for Daniyal. He wrote a will to make sure Daniyal was raised by his mother in Peshawar, far from Lahore.

Khalid looked over at Farhad, signaling that he was ready to start. He whispered something in his ear and went to the microphone, then pulled out a set of keys and read the house number aloud, repeating it twice. The first man in line stepped forward and walked up to the wooden panel and stood behind it. Mrs. Seema Khan slowly made her way to the front with her two children in tow right behind her. She kept her head down but made sure to glance over at her husband who was at the end of the line. One of her children kept crying aloud, "Mummy . . . mummy . . . where are we going? Where is Papa? Where is papa?" Mrs. Khan made sure to turn her children away from the direction of her husband and stepped up to the podium, looking directly at Khalid who held her house keys in his right palm.

"I don't think I can do this Khalid bhai," Mrs. Khan said as she took the set of keys from his hand.

"Of course, you can, Seema. You're just frightened because you are the first one up here. Afzal is waiting for you. He's a doctor and he is on duty tonight. Just get on home and put the children to bed first. Your husband will be back in the morning. Don't ask any more questions, nah. We have more men waiting."

Mrs. Khan craned her neck and caught her husband's eyes, then wiped her own on the ends of her dupatta. Now she could feel herself being pushed from behind by the other women and stepped behind the wooden panel with her house keys clutched tightly in her palm. People let her through, but she could hear a few voices chuckle, "What an odd couple. . . . Seema and Afzal. Wonder how the night will end!" Seema Khan stood behind the panel with her children right behind her and saw Afzal standing there in silence. She handed him her keys to the house and followed him to his car parked in the dirt road alongside Khalid's house. It was pitch dark and Seema had a hard time balancing the children while walking in her heels. She almost fell a few times as the folds of her shalwar got caught under her heels. "It is a beautiful night, isn't it?" said Afzal cheerfully. Seema did not look up from the ground and thought about her servants at home and how they knew not to ask questions and sleep at the back of the house tonight, away from the front steps where Seema walked into her home with her children and Afzal, her neighbor a few doors down in the compound—her husband's doctor.

"Well now that the first woman has left the tent . . . let's get started," said Khalid. "Hopefully no one is missing, and we can get on with the night." The crowd in the tent looked around to see if anyone was missing. Khalid now went faster calling out the house numbers into the microphone. He hurried the women up quickly to the front of the tent and had Farhad grab them by their arms to move them along.

"Mona. Mona Habib. Does anyone see her?" someone said in the tent.

"I see Mr. Habib in the line. Not sure where she is."

"I think it is their first time . . . right? They're here just for a few months in the summer. Don't they live abroad?"

"Yes, the husband works in Chicago as an engineer and Mona's parents live in Lahore."

Mona Habib did not want to take part in this exchange and instead hid behind the pink bougainvillea flowers cascading down from the compound wall in the western side of the house facing the back alley. She had been married to Iqbal for a few years and held onto their daughter Reema in her arms. When Khalid called out their house number, she looked right at Iqbal from behind the vines to see what he would do. He darted his eyes quickly around the tent but could not see her. Then Iqbal took his hands out of his pant pockets and crossed them across the chest.

"Mona Habib," several people said, "Mona Habib. Mona Habib."

Khalid looked over at Iqbal and shook his head. "We are going to take the Habibs off our list for tonight. Husbands please make sure to talk to your wives before coming to the party." Farhad ran over and gave Iqbal the house keys who then wandered around the tent looking for his wife and daughter.

"Can I go home with Ahmed instead? I know my keys are still in the bowl. I can pick them out. I want to go home with him," bellowed Haniya Baig. All the women turned to look at her but had already recognized her baying voice. Haniya was a tall and lanky woman with long, thin black hair that went past her knees. Her aquiline face was formidable, her dusky skin belied her upper caste and her small rounded eyes pierced through men like splinters.

Khalid turned to look at her with caution. "Wives cannot pick who they want to go home with. That is not allowed." Khalid then stepped down from the podium and went right up to Haniya and whispered fiercely in front of her face, "How could you do this? Humiliate your husband? With your children in front of you. Sharing your desire for Ahmed in public like this."

"Really, Khalid? What are we doing here tonight? Please explain this to me. How about you and Zara explain to all of us what this night is about and why our husbands brought us here?" replied Haniya. Although everyone under the tent knew the answer to this question well, it was Khalid who would get to decide how to run the numbers.

"Ms. Baig, if you do not like how we run things here . . . you and your husband are free to go" replied Khalid with a heightened sense of politeness.

"Guess I will wait in line with the other women," responded Haniya and walked away with her two sons, Ishaan and Shezaan.

"Right, I will make sure to keep your name on the list Mrs. Baig"

"Haniya," piped her husband Abid walking toward them. Abid looked nervously at Khalid but then ducked his head as he heard people in the crowd say things like, "What is your wife doing" and "Looks like she knows what she wants." Abid returned back to his spot in the queue.

"Well, I guess we can move on," said Khalid, clearing his throat. "House number 829?"

"Here," a woman's voice said, and Khalid nodded his head. The crowd went back to its hushed murmurs and the children were now mostly asleep on the floor of the tent or in the garden. Khalid began to call more and more house numbers and the earlier feeling of agitation dissipated as the night moved on. The men kept coming forward from the line and standing behind the wooden panel as the women made their way to the front, collecting their children along the way. There was a quiet lull in the tent as the crowd lessened in numbers. Khalid looked up from the podium every once in a while, to see who was left in the crowd. He wet his lips, not looking up from the podium, and read the next number—"House number 723." The man who came forward in the line was Mr. Iftikhar Naqvi and the woman who came up to the front was his sister-in-law, who also lived in the same compound, Maira Malik, the younger sister of his wife, Ateebah Naqvi. Iftikhar and Maira grinned at each other nervously unsure of what to do next. Khalid looked at both sets of family members in the crowd, noticing that they stood apart from each other.

"Maira," Khalid said, "Maira Malik."

"Seems like no one would have predicted this match."

"How can he do this with his own sister-in-law."

"There are no rules against it either."

"They are in-laws and not blood related."

Mr. Atif Malik held his breath as his wife Maira came forward and started walking toward the wooden panel. "How could she," he said to himself, denouncing his wife for forsaking him.

"There she goes," said the women in the crowd, "Go, Maira. We're all next."

Atif watched his wife come around the wooden panel with his children and his brother-in-law waiting for her. By now, the other men in line looked around at Atif, "Get up there Atif and bring your wife back." Some of the men in line started laughing, "Atif?"

"Atif," said the man behind him. "Just let her go. It will be your turn soon. They say the Pakistani government will shut down these beevi badalna games soon in the next months. The mullahs have teamed up with the MPs and the military and are calling this haram. Just wait your turn . . . you never know when you will get this chance again."

   The Louisville Review

"What zealots and hypocrites!" shouted back the petulant man a few feet behind Atif. "Everything is haram for them. What about the villages? Will they go after the uneducated grown men marrying young girls? Next thing you know we will become Afghanistan and women will be required to wear a burka everywhere. Look at the Taliban walking around with guns and killing the innocent even today. For what? Life was better for us under the Shahs and the Khans. We have always had nikah mutah in our culture."

"Some places have already quit beevi badalna. Islamabad has banned it."

"Nothing but hypocrites in Slackistan," shouted back the stout old man, "Pack of fools."

"Atif bhai . . . it will be alright. Just get back in line and stay the course."

"I wish they'd hurry," said the men behind Atif.

"They are almost through. Atif you will be next." By now, his wife was gone and at home with his brother-in-law. Atif also wished they'd hurry up. Khalid called out the next house number and motioned Atif to come forward. Zarina Wahlid came forward just as Atif was making his way to the wooden panel. She pulled him aside and said, "Don't be nervous Atif. We still have a lot of time." Zarina was one of the few women who did not have children and Atif felt much more relieved and took her house keys in his hand. They walked back to his car with Zarina walking in lock step behind him in her pink embroidered saree. After Atif and Zarina walked away, Khalid took a pause and a deep breath. He looked around the tent and saw a few stragglers left, even though it was now past midnight.

"I have been doing this for almost three years," said Bashir, who was one of the last in line, adjusting his hair with a small black comb that he tucked into his back-pant pocket.

"Okay, gentleman," said Khalid. For a few minutes, nobody moved. Then Farhad rattled the bowl with the last few sets of keys. "House Number 626."

"Who lives in 626?"

"Who is it?"

"Is it the Johars?"

"Is it the Lateefs?"

It was a young beautiful woman who walked up when her house number was called. She had golden brown hair that looked like gossamer, granite green eyes, and plumb lips. Her oval face was outlined in a beautiful blue silk dupatta that hid the dangling gold jhumka earrings that twirled and pirouetted as she made her way to the front.

"Oh, it's her . . . the Afghani woman that Mr. Johar brought home from the brothel."

Khalid looked over at Farhad, "Go get him . . . the next man in line."

People began to look around to see which lucky man was going home with the Afghani.

Mr. Habib was standing there in the queue with his head held down. He was twice her age, bald, stocky and with daughters the same age as her.

"You can't do that Khalid. She is too young," shouted the women in the tent.

"You know the night will be short for her Khalid!" laughed another woman.

"Be a good sport Khalid and pass her onto the next one. She does not understand Urdu. She speaks Pashto."

"All of us would do the same. Pass her on Khalid."

"Please be quiet!" Khalid shouted at the women, and then he looked over at Mr. Habib who appeared tired and confused under the veil of shouting women. Then Khalid looked behind him and saw men who were not that much younger than Mr. Habib.

"Farhad . . . come here. You go home with the Afghani woman, Mrs. Johar," said Khalid. "I will talk to Asma . . . just go now."

"But Khalid . . . you know I cannot," protested Farhad. "I am here only to help. Asma will kill me. She knows this is haram."

"Don't worry about her or the children," responded Khalid, "I will tell her that you stayed late to help clean up the house. Just go now and you can be back home soon."

Farhad looked over at the Afghani woman and motioned for her to step behind the same wooden panel that he had put together a few hours ago. He reminded himself that he needs to return and bring back the wooden chilman to his home before Asma starts to ask questions in the morning. With nervous hands, Farhad grabbed the elbows of the Afghani woman and looked back at Khalid for one last reassurance.

Khalid nodded and turned to the remaining people in the tent, "Well everyone. That was not as fast as I hoped it would be. I think it is time for us to stop now. I don't think there are any more households left." Although he was chuckling at this admission, Khalid grew weary and just wanted to go back home with Zara and wait for the morning.

"What about us Khalid! We have been standing and waiting here all night."

Khalid looked over at the remaining men and women, an uneven number with more men than women. Khalid did not know any of them well and had only seem them in passing when he went for his evening walks around the compound.

"We're still here. Noor and Fatima. There's Abdul and Hameed."

"We need our turn Khalid! It's not fair!"

"It is getting late people," said Khalid regretfully.

"I have no children Khalid. At least let me go," said Noor unabashedly.

"Why do we even need Khalid to draw house numbers?"

"That's right! We don't need him."

"How many of us are left?"

"There's five men and three women. Abdul, Hameed, Arshad, Maqbool, and Sameer. Then there is Noor, Fatima, and Yasmine."

"All right then," said Khalid, "why don't you figure it out yourselves."

"What about your wife Zara? Zara Begum? Zara Bhabhi?"

"Yes, why not? Ready to join us Zara?" the women asked.

"Listen everybody," said Khalid, glancing over furtively at his wife. Zara on the other hand was delighted by the women's comments.

"Ready, Zara?" the women asked as if they were about to venture off to a picnic together.

"Remember that we all have to return to our homes by early morning. We only have a few hours left. We cannot wake up the children. We cannot let any of the older children see us come in and leave in the morning. We must be discreet."

Zara looked at the women and nodded her head. Khalid was turning angry and was scowling at the women. He almost knocked over the wooden chilman. The women took a collective breath and moved to guard Zara from her husband.

"Zara, let's go," said the women defiantly.

"Zara?" pleaded Khalid when she walked past. Zara hesitated for a moment, looked directly at her husband and pursed her lips. Then she turned away with the women and made her way to the other side of the tent. At the last minute, Zara stopped to check her purse to see if the house keys were with her since they had locked up the empty house when everyone walked out to the tent. The lights were still on in the house. The servants were outside cleaning up the tables, washing the giant metal cooking pots with the well water, and sweeping the dirt on the stairs leading onto the veranda. "Zara! Zara!" yelled Khalid.

She fumbled around for the keys, bringing them out with her hand raised in the air above her head so Khalid could see that she had them.

The small crowd grew quiet, waiting to see what Khalid would do. "I hope Zara still comes," whispered Noor so that Khalid could not hear her.

"This is not the way it is supposed to be, Zara! This is not the way, Zara!" screamed Khalid at the top of his lungs. Then Khalid sat down at the plastic table near the podium.

"It will be okay," said Abdul as he patted Khalid on the back while leaving with the crowd.

Khalid sat in the middle of the Bedouin tent with his head bent into his folded hands. The empty glass bowl sat next to him on the table. "It isn't fair," he said to himself. He looked over to his own home and saw the silhouette of Zara in their bedroom. Then the lights slowly shut across the entire house, one by one. The only light on now was the one in his son's bedroom.

"Go to bed, Daniyal. Go to bed," said Khalid as he closed his eyes and set to sleep. He could hear the azaan from the Badshahi mosque and the sound of lorries rambling down distant roads. The early morning fog was rising as a thin layer of sunlight crept across the light blue dawn, the songs of the morning larks dangling overhead.

Gabrielle LeJeune

Sweep the Sun off the Roof

Frank Todd Holland carried the blue of twilight on his white shirt as he made his way home after another day of work. Once inside, he slouched in his favorite chair and muttered to himself until dinner was ready. His glare lasted while he sat at the table and ate. It was Friday, payday, and though he hadn't as yet cashed his paycheck, Holland knew most of it would go to his family. He sat silently with his wife and children, glancing up now and then, knowing they would never go away.

The following day while walking his dog, a Boston terrier with one blind eye, Holland found his son eating wild blackberries in a vacant lot overgrown with weeds. "Here," he said, reaching in his pocket for a napkin, "wipe your face, or your mother will think I smacked you in the mouth."

Sunday passed without another sour word, but when Monday came, his youngest daughter ran home crying about a crowd of blue jays raucously cawing, wildly flying from branch to branch under a canopy of trees. The birds frightened the child, who taking another way home from school, ran through the thicket. With blue feathers and green leaves in her hair, she rushed over to her father and sat on his lap, wrapping her arms around him.

Taking her arms from around his neck, and holding her by the shoulders, he told her that she had done the right thing. "Turn around and be afraid to walk forward, and you'll be turning around for the rest of your life. Walk through and maybe you'll have a chance at something better than what you have now." That was all he said on the matter.

Later that night, however, he caught hold of his eldest child and said, "You look like you're working in the back of a truck stop. Fourteen years old and you already look like a tramp." She screamed, calling to her mother for help while Holland got his hand tangled in her teased hair, held in place with Aquanet.

Walking his dog, Holland passed dilapidated homes rented out to West Virginians who were still traveling north up from Appalachia to find work in the steel mills. Although most of the factories had been closed for years, leaving isolated, poorly lit industrial areas, the impoverished were still coming.

"Have you noticed?" Holland said to his wife later on that night. "The girls from West Virginia, no older than fourteen or fifteen years old are still getting it on with the poor city blacks? What do they call their kids? Mulattoes, that's what they call them, up and down every street. Soon, there won't be one white bastard in all of Cuyahoga County, not one."

"Meanwhile," he continued, "I've got to listen to that old man sitting on his porch hacking, spitting up sludge, trying to take a clear breath, trying to get the coal out of his lungs. The black dust is embedded in his pores and makes his skin look ashen. Have you noticed? Even in winter, he keeps his shirt open in the hope that it will help him breathe easier."

"I went to visit Melissa the other day," his wife began, talking about the family downstairs, warily engaging her husband. "I thought I was seeing things. She brought a pan of cornbread out to the porch for her kin. In ten seconds, there wasn't one crumb left, ten seconds later and not one crumb left." Suddenly, his wife flushed with embarrassment when her husband's eyes narrowed at her choice of company. Suddenly, she looked away, crossing the kitchen floor as if she needed an ingredient for dinner that was clear across the room.

Holland just looked at his wife, thinking this is not the woman I wanted to marry, this is not the woman I thought I knew, not when his wife often pushed him off her body, though he had tried in a half-hearted way to please her. This is not the life I wanted, he thought, not when on payday he felt a tug on every pocket of his polyester pants. As it was, it was becoming an effort to move, to put one foot in front of the other just to make it through the day.

As a youth, Holland was awkward, stumbled, fumbled, and fell down frequently. At twelve years of age, he was in the habit of punching trees with thick, rough bark until his knuckles were bruised and bloodied, letting the wounds scab over before punching more trees in an effort to look menacing if anyone tried to pick a fight with him.

But as he grew into a young man he was thought of as good looking, and once he knew how to handle himself, he left one pretty girl for another. He went for the city girls of Cleveland, girls whose mothers took them to Halle's for lunch in the Geranium Room. But he had only heard about the cavernous room with a high ceiling, green stems as tall as trees growing up the walls, and giant red geraniums in full bloom.

He could only imagine the fabulous stores in downtown Cleveland. Finally venturing in, he was dazzled by the displays of apparel he never saw anyone wear, at least no one he knew. His clothes were shabby, his hair was dirty, and he held expressions that never brightened his face. Worse still, any time someone asked, "May I help you?" he only heard, "What are you doing here? What is someone like you doing here?"

There was an older saleslady who took an interest in him, who stood behind a counter of ties and told him to try on some of the clothes for young men. Soon, she was beginning to use her employee discount to buy him a modest wardrobe. And while at first he thought it was his imagination, he definitely could hear the nearly imperceptible sound of purring whenever she wore a knit dress and brought her body close to him.

When he learned that the department stores were closing, Frank Todd Holland was enraged that Cleveland was losing Halle's, Higbee's, and the May Company. He thought if the city wants to look desolate, he would make the city look worse than it already was.

Caught in the act, he was picked up for vandalism before he could browse the aisles, possibly for the last time, just to look at new clothes on smart-looking mannequins. Rather than feel sorry for the downtown's loss of elegant, fair-haired shoppers, he thought of buying a pig's head from the West Side Market and mailing it to the mayor. It was, however, far too expensive and would cost way too much to send.

Briefly disciplined, he was then picked up for having thrown another brick through another store window. Holland soon began to think of himself as a juvenile delinquent. He was handed a broom and pointed to a flight of steps that led to the flat rooftop of the detention facility. There, on the very top of the building, he was told to sweep the sun off the roof. Every day thereafter, he was given the same instructions.

"Sweep the sun off the roof." It was a work detail that to him was outrageous, and clearly meant to show the young man how pointless his life would be if he continued to follow the path he was on. Every day he was told to sweep the sun off the roof—not just on bright, sunny days, but on cloudy days, in the rain, when it was snowing and once when the sky opened up, hailing ice the size of mothballs, the size he used to shape from yellow snow he found around trees, the size of the round ice balls he threw at his classmates as they made their way home from school. He knew if he didn't change his life now, it would be spent either in futile acts of destruction or in equally futile acts of forced repentance, both unacceptable to him when all along he wanted to be a different sort of man.

He longed for those days when he went out with the city girls of Cleveland. He missed the feel of their dresses, the shades of their hair, soft to the touch, and the smell of their skin, bathed every day. They all laughed easily and knew enough to blot their lipstick before giving him a kiss. Now they were all gone when there was no reason to come downtown anymore.

Having swept the sun off the roof for exactly a year, Holland was released from juvenile detention and began to be aware of the local girls, aware that while they may be second best, he wouldn't have to try so hard to know what they wanted.

Soon, he became interested in a girl who lived three blocks away. She also laughed easily and even seemed to know some joy in life. He wanted those qualities in a wife. He didn't want a girl who felt the drudgery of existence in every step she took. He didn't want a wife who started her day with despair, leaving him with the burden of a mate, tired and worn out before she was even seventeen.

As it was, after he married, Holland knew that he had made too many wrong turns in life, too many mistakes—staying in Ohio, staying in the buckle of the Rustbelt. Finding he had no talent for anything special, he got work at a store called Drug World on the west side of Cleveland.

He began stocking the shelves, toiling his way up from assistant to manager in a brief period of time, going to work every day on the Rapid Transit and coming home to his wife and children, who were expecting him to keep them clothed, housed and, in his opinion, excessively well-fed.

And for a while at least he accepted his fate as he found it. Until the day when a gun was pushed in his face, letting the thieves escape with bags of drugs and money. Without ever firing a shot, the thugs left spots of Holland's blood dripping on his white patent leather shoes, saying, "No, I can't describe any of you" and "No, I didn't see which way you were going."

He wiped the sweat and blood off his face where he had felt the muzzle of a gun grinding against his skull. He obeyed their every demand for cash and drugs. "This better be the good shit!" They kept saying while the pharmacist grimly assured the delinquents that they'd been given only the very best painkillers and that they could leave content in that knowledge.

After that episode, Holland handled his children and wife roughly and treated the world in a different sort of way. He resented that his wife required a sizable part of his pay from him. He was no longer polite to customers who thought he was expected to help, saying it wasn't part of his job description. So when the older patrons asked questions of the medication they were prescribed, he held the bottle to their waxy ears and shaking it violently, drowned out every additional query they might happen to have. Moreover, he pushed slow-walking stock boys aside with his shoulder and told cashiers who rushed up to him with problems of pricing to get out of his way.

The waitress who served him coffee in the morning stood behind the counter, also serving him coffee after work. "You know if the squad car hadn't been facing the new RTA station at 101st maybe they would have caught them." The young lady, who had the mere beginnings of varicose veins, was starting to catch his eye. "They're worried about vandals destroying the new station," she said.

"That couldn't be the closest precinct," he said to her. "But there are drugs being sold all the way to Lakewood. I see them. I see them all the time."

"Except for winter, when it's too cold for even the dealers to be outside," they said at the same time, giving them both a moment to relax and laugh in the warmth of each other's company.

"Look, look there. They're right across the avenue." He said, also seeing the ones like him, who were waiting for buses that never came according to schedule, especially in winter, when the poor, would-be riders could no longer endure the frustration of waiting and would instead decide to walk away.

Recalling his youth, he remembered the phrase: sweep the sun off the roof. Even when he worked diligently, he was prodded by the guards to work faster, taunted and told he missed a spot. He nearly fell off the building one day when the sun got in his eyes. And when winter came and the days were short, the youths were awakened at first light, taken outside, and other than the occasional break, were brought back in for the night only when it was turning dark.

Later that day, Holland didn't go home but rather spent the first of many nights with the waitress. He got off work one hour before her shift was over and spent many calm, peaceful hours in her company. Sometimes she asked him over for dinner, or sometimes he would see that she was so tired, at his urging, he'd order take-out, pay for it and end the night at her place.

Night after night, he saw her uniform, soaking in the bathroom sink, a white uniform that had gotten so filthy with spills and messes, she'd have to wash it out every night and hang it up on the clothesline above her bathtub to have it dry by morning. He was convinced that sooner or later she would ask him to wash it out, but she didn't. She dragged herself to the bathroom and every night without saying a word, washed out her uniform, never asking anything of him.

However, the affair came to a sudden end when, falling down on an icy patch of sidewalk one day, when the temperature in Cleveland was five degrees below zero, he slipped and broke his nose and a variety of bones, which, despite the doctor's reassurances, completely ruined the perfect features of his face. Suddenly, he was wearing a bandage that was so large it looked as if he was protecting a beak. He'd never have anything to offer a woman, he thought, now that his looks were gone.

He spent most of his time walking his half-blind dog while he collected disability checks, until one day he was surprised to hear his wife call for a taxi. She was going to the hospital to give birth to their fourth child and second son. "I would have gone with you," he called from the window.

"Why should I think you'll do anything for me?" she shouted back. "Why should I expect anything from you?" In the meantime, while she was still protesting, he was thinking, she is the one who will have to find work now. He couldn't be expected to provide enough to keep his family alive, not now, not when he had a broken face and couldn't stop his hands from shaking ever since the robbery at Drug World.

He had to take a leave of absence. He had to get away, escape his family's clutching, grubbing, tugging at his pockets for his very last buck. He could have used the extra money, but didn't steal the good drugs when he had a chance, not when he didn't want to risk being locked up again, feeling as though life had no meaning.

Even so, his wife continued to ask why he didn't take what the thieves left behind when Holland had access to the pharmacy. She asked why he didn't sell those drugs as soon as they were in his hands and blame their disappearance on the pharmacist, who Holland could say took advantage of the situation. Certainly, there must be some addicts out there who come in out of the cold, looking for drugs, thinking they found heaven in a store called Drug World.

He went for a walk one night and picked out a car in an area so poor, it had no stop signs or streetlights. The dog blind in one eye followed him. His youngest daughter followed him. Later that night, she watched her father hotwire a red Chevy. However, when Holland looked up at her and she in turn saw, in the spark of wires, pure hatred in his eyes, she recoiled at the sight and ran all the way home.

He set out on the road with his Boston terrier at his side but once he realized that he had nowhere to go, once he realized that he was almost out of gas, he abandoned the car and walked back to his half-rented house with no one at the door to greet him.

Nothing was said except, "He's home again" in a cheerless tone of voice when one of his children caught sight of him. No one wanted him there. That much he knew.

"Sweep the sun off the roof," was all he could hear in his thoughts. All he could do was watch his family, in his every waking hour, watch his hands shake, knowing he could do nothing for them. Even walking his dog became a nuisance to him and was just now beginning to loosen his grip on the leash.

Holland went back to the waitress, who said he was as handsome as ever, and said she couldn't tell his nose and bones in his face were ever broken. He began spending most of his time with her, taking off her shoes and stockings, rubbing her feet, trying to relieve her suffering when she was standing all day.

One night, he watched her collapse onto the sofa. And in a surprising act, he slipped off her uniform, sat on the side of the tub and washed it out, scrubbing the stains vigorously. Seeing that her uniform was so much whiter when he cleaned it, he took a step back, admired his efforts, when there it was, the white uniform without a single stain, hanging on the clothesline, only the cleanest of water dripping into her bathtub.

He took a look in the mirror of the medicine cabinet and was pleased by what he saw. As long as he was in her apartment, in her presence, as long as she asked nothing from him, as long as his family couldn't find him, he could finally be giving and gracious, the kind of man he always wanted to be.

Lynn Gordon

SMALL, BEAUTIFUL THINGS

Joseph went about his days with admirable dispatch. Mornings, he walked eight blocks to the office building where, under a trembling blue light, he spent hours producing what the company called visuals: charts, graphs, montages, collages, and artfully doctored photographs.

What distinguished his work were the hand-done touches. On computerized charts he lettered the captions and call-outs in India ink, copying fonts from a large book he kept on hand, and occasionally added small embellishments at the corners of a page. His work was acknowledged even by his supervisor, who once or twice said, "It would have been fine to have the computer spit it all out, but it's fine this way, too." Joseph felt sure that his visuals drew particular interest from people who saw them at meetings, that they popped out at people the way a hand-addressed envelope did in the mail.

One Tuesday, a co-worker named Ryan came in the door of his solitary office. "So this is where you squirrel yourself away. What is that you're doing?" Ryan stepped closer to Joseph's drafting table. "What kind of a pen is that?"

Joseph needed to concentrate, but weeks had passed since anyone had stopped by his office, so he turned from his work and responded politely.

Ryan listened to Joseph for a moment, nodded, and said, "Old school. I get it." And he left the office in a light mist of condescension.

Per his Saturday routine, Joseph dialed his father and waited through eight or nine rings.

"Is that you, Joseph?" rumbled his father. A loud clunk followed, as of the telephone being dropped. Then his father again: "I thought you would call earlier."

"How are you, Dad?"

"Not now."

Joseph enunciated, conscious of each outsized movement of his lips. "How. Are. You."

"Were you busy with Rowena, too busy to call?"

"No." He had to shout. "I'm not busy. How. Are. You."

"What about the job? You still at the bank?" A coughing fit ensued.

These calls never lasted long. His father's deafness seemed to be heading into dementia, a known correlation.

Troubled, and half-dreading the call from his sister that would surely come soon, Joseph took a handful of peanuts from a bowl on the counter, slid open the glass door to his patio, and settled himself on a vinyl-strapped lounge chair. He selected one peanut and balanced it carefully on his left leg just above the knee, the pale shell a contrast to his dark pants. He leaned back and waited.

At first, he darted his eyes around the patio, searching into the branches that hung over from outside the walls, probing his lone camellia bush. After a time, a hummingbird motored in to sip from his potted fuchsia. It arrived and departed several times, whirring and twitching.

Joseph turned his eyes back toward the tree branches. He didn't dare let his mind wander; he might upset the peanut or miss a sighting. The next time he glanced at the fuchsia, the hummingbird was not there.

He thought about Ryan's visit to his office, and about his remark: "Old school." Ryan was one of the numerous younger people who inhabited the company. Joseph, who was over fifty, had made an effort to dress like the rest, abandoning the white shirts and foulard ties from his long-ago days at the bank, but he knew himself to be different, perhaps unbridgeably apart from the coders and tech heads and geeks, or whatever they called themselves.

A rustle caught his attention. A jay had landed in the camellia and was flailing for balance. Joseph made himself into a block of sandstone. He breathed scarcely enough to oxygenate his blood.

The jay stayed where she was, her toes clutching a thin branch. She cocked one eye toward Joseph. Joseph, who had no doubt the bird was studying the peanut, breathed even more shallowly than before.

After a long stand-off, Joseph gave in and tossed the peanut to the ground. The jay hesitated, twisting her head to look downward. After a moment she flew over the wall and was gone.

The call came as Joseph was trimming his moustache. He set down the moustache scissors and went to answer, almost calling Tracy by name before she spoke a word.

Tracy got right to it: "You talked to him?" She wanted a debrief after every conversation, every week.

"How are you? Don't you want to know how I am?"

"We'll get to that. But how was he? What did you think?"

"Well." Joseph touched a finger to his moustache, patting the trimmed part and then the still-scraggly place near the corner of his mouth. "He doesn't hear very well; you know that."

"What else is new," said Tracy. "How's his mind? Was he on the floor killing moths?"

Joseph was reluctant to inform on his father, but he knew Tracy would worm things out of him eventually. "We didn't talk all that long. He asked about the bank again."

"Yesss. It's not just the odd slip-up. He's done that three times now."

"You're keeping a tally?"

"Anything else? Because I've been researching places. I have to be ready to act."

"Please. Please take it easy. He's not hurting anyone." Again, he touched the overgrown hairs at the corner of his mouth.

"What else? Come on."

He cast about for a detail, any detail, of the unmemorable conversation. "He did ask about Ramona, which is reasonable. We only broke it off two months ago."

"But again with the bank. That smacks of memory loss. Disorientation."

Joseph waited without saying anything. He didn't mention that his father had said Rowena instead of Ramona.

"All right, Joseph. How are you? What's up in your bachelor world?"

He hadn't thought she would ask. "Well, new projects at work. I'm trying color washes on a photo piece." Silence. "And I'm doing something new at home. I'm training a jay to eat peanuts from my hand." He said it, and at once wondered why he had.

"A blue jay. That's what you're doing. And I'm running around like a half-wit, even though I have two daughters and a job at the blood bank, looking at assisted living versus continuous care versus what-all. There are a thousand versions of the living afterlife."

He stirred sympathy into his voice. He was the one living far away while everything fell on Tracy. "I'm glad you're looking into it. I just don't want Dad getting shut up when he's doing all right."

"You should see what those women are like—it's mostly women.

They're all dolled up to look maternal and corporate at the same time, they show you around, waving to everyone in sight so you can see how doggone friendly it is. You can hardly get a decent answer."

"Mmm." Joseph hated hearing these details. He stooped to pick a thread from the carpet.

"Every time you ask a question, like what about laundry, they draw themselves up all holy and say *that's for the family to handle.*"

"He's all right at home, isn't he? Give him some time."

"Right. Well, good luck with your starling." The dial tone sang in relief.

Joseph returned to the bathroom, where his moustache snippers waited, pointed and gleaming. He had bought them special at a cutler's. He would trim the remaining bits of hair, make a final pass all the way across, and his moustache would be left flawless.

He had gotten the idea about blue jays from Ramona. She'd mentioned one time that her father had done it, had reached the point where he could sit in his yard and a neighborhood jay would fly straight to his hand, even when he didn't have a peanut.

Just recently, Joseph had decided to take on the same endeavor. It was both possible and finite, and it offered the prospect of a kinship between himself and another being. He might bring together two unlinked members of the universe.

The first time the jay retrieved a peanut from the ground beside his lounge chair, Joseph mentioned it to his father.

"I have a bird who came to get a peanut from me. In my patio." Even as he said the words, he felt a brilliance behind his eyes.

"A bird," said his father. "What kind of bird eats peanuts? Not sparrows." His voice was musing and rational.

The entire call, in fact, went well, given the hindrance of his father's deafness. Joseph reported this to Tracy, but the news scarcely registered.

"I'm narrowing it down," she said, with a heavy breath. "You'd think it would go faster, but suddenly Melissa isn't keeping anything down—*that* takes up time." Melissa was the younger daughter.

"But there isn't any hurry. He sounded good, even said he made himself oatmeal."

"Instant. Just tear open the package. And I had to drag her off to the clinic; you have to make sure. So one of these days I'll have a decision."

"I'm sorry she's sick."

"When the day comes, you'll need to chip in."

One day, he inked a small portrait of a jay in the margin beside a bar graph. He liked to do small, beautiful things, and he lingered over the thin white brow and white throat. It was a challenge to make the eyeball stand out from the black feathers around it; he ended by outlining a tiny reflection of light in the eye.

For the first time in his years at the company, the supervisor rejected his work. He had given Joseph a peering look and said something about going overboard, and maybe it was time to cut out the frills.

At home that evening, Joseph arranged tomato slices on a plate and dressed them with vinaigrette and Italian parsley. He ate his concoction while drinking red wine but found himself half-wishing for a cigarette. He'd never smoked; that had been Ramona's habit. He remembered the smell.

After finishing the tomatoes, he poured himself a second glass of wine and went to the living room to look at magazines; he had a small backlog of *Smithsonian* and *Architectural Digest*. Before long, his mind went hollow over the glossy pictures, and the wine addled his vision. The room was growing dim and he did not bother to turn on a light. There was no mistaking that his job, his way of doing things, was under threat.

He remembered the old times at the bank, where his days were devoid of lettering, pen-and-ink, or any sort of drawing. Artwork had been limited to a single wall sculpture of divergent metal rods. In those days he had no choice about hours or how to dress.

It came back to him that the branch had had many customers of retirement age. Yes. He took another wavering swallow of wine. Puffy old people with canes, gaunt people with their skin hanging loose. He could picture them now. On the fifth of each month, the people would line up fifty or sixty deep, wanting to cash their Social Security checks.

Many of the customers read the plate on his desk and called him by name. Every day, it seemed, a woman would say, "Morning, Joseph. Isn't the wind something today?" or a man would nod and make a crack about how much cash he planned to withdraw. ATMs were not widespread yet, and everybody came in.

The room grew darker. A glimmer washed in from a distant streetlight. They lived on the edge, some of those people. A ten-dollar overdraw fee could devastate them. He used to waive fees left and right for those frayed old people.

Still his job went on. He created visuals, taking pains not to overdo. When Ryan wandered in once again, he found Joseph preparing a chart on the computer.

"Hey. How's it doing?" Ryan dragged a stool between his legs and sat.

Joseph looked up, nodded. He took in Ryan's khaki pants and black turtleneck, the thin face with its chin bristles.

"Doing my job. Same old." He let his hands lie still in his lap.

"Brought you something. I thought you could use it." There was an odd glitter in Ryan's eyes. He held out a small paper bag.

Joseph rustled the bag open and slid out the contents: a rubber stamp and a pad with green ink. The stamp's image looked like a ball with four other balls stuck into it.

"It's silicon, bonded with hydrogen. Tetravalent, right?"

Joseph nodded, glancing at his computer screen, at Ryan, and then at the rubber stamp. "Thanks." He realized he was still nodding.

"Okay, then." Ryan slapped his shoulder and strode out the door into the hallway. The words "have a good one" reached Joseph's ears.

He sat pushing his fingertips together. At last, he opened the tin lid of the ink pad, applied the stamp, and pressed out the image on a piece of scrap paper. Balls. A silicon molecule. It was the wrong thing at the wrong time. And it was patronizing. He stamped the image several more times, fainter and fainter until the ink wore off.

Progress was happening with the jay. Becoming inured to Joseph's presence, she flew down to eat peanuts from the ground beside him. At first, she would merely pluck up a peanut and fly away with it. Later, she began eating the nuts right there on the ground. He liked to watch her hack into the shell and swallow the peanut with a visible flexion of her throat. It was a great satisfaction to see her eat peanut after peanut or carry one away and then quickly return for more.

It was a banner day when she swooped down for a peanut he'd placed on his leg. She seemed to accept his presence as if he were a tree branch. When she landed on his knee, he felt the small scratch of her claws and rejoiced.

That evening, on his living room couch, he picked up his phone and held it in his lap. When the sun dropped low, he switched on a light and returned to the couch and the phone. At last, he made a call.

"Joseph? What's up, are you all right?"

His throat iced over. He pushed out some words: "More than all right." That was the wrong way to begin. He started again. "How are you? I just wanted to tell you something."

"What is it?" As she spoke, he saw her in his mind: the dark hair in a silver clip, the blade of her jaw, a cigarette between her lips.

"You're doing all right, though?"

"Joseph, just tell me." She was almost certainly smoking, little lines rucking the skin around her mouth as she drew in the smoke.

"I've been training a jay. Like your father, with peanuts."

"You have." A slow, smoky silence, during which Joseph forced himself to hang on. "What made you do that?"

"I wanted to let you know, so you could tell your father, well, today she—that's the jay—she took a peanut I had set on my leg. I was sitting down, of course, and I couldn't help thinking of your father. I thought I'd tell you."

Her voice became quiet. "Joseph, remember we had a decision. You remember. And I'll call you if anything changes. Really, I will."

With that, he was left with the unbending telephone, in his lighted room that held no trace of smoke.

At first, Joseph couldn't tell who was on the line. Only when the coughing began did he realize.

"Dad, how are you? Are you there?" His father calling him, not the other way around, and it wasn't even a Saturday.

"Jose..." There was something wrong. He seemed to be choking.

"Dad. Do you need me to call 9-1-1? Can you get your breath?" Joseph's legs were bending. Soon he was sitting on the floor. During the next muffled seconds, he thought of hanging up and trying the ER in Denver, but that wouldn't be possible unless his father hung up first.

"Do something, Joseph." He was crying, that was it, he was crying. "She wants to take me away. To an awful . . ." A sharp breath. "To some kind of joint."

"Dad. My God."

"I can't take anything with me. I'll have to wear a uniform, and they make you do things." More choking.

Joseph didn't bother to contest any of it. The floor felt very hard under him. He pulled on his shoelace so that the knot fell apart and kept pulling while the shoelace dug a groove in his hand.

He had to calm himself before talking to Tracy. He went out to his patio and reclined in the lounge chair. A red fuchsia bloom dangled from its hanging pot, glared at him. He closed his eyes against it. After a while, he felt a thin breeze against his face and throat.

Tracy had finally done it. She was taking their father from his home. Tracy and Joseph had lived there with him, and their mother. Joseph heard swishing sounds, perhaps from the branches and leaves that overhung his patio wall. The wind was getting stronger.

From somewhere over the wall came a cry, a shriek. He knew it was his jay.

Tracy got straight down to business. "It's time. Did you know he let a pan melt on his stove last week? And where have you been while I had to figure everything out? Tell me that."

"I'm sorry," he said, even as a downward pressure attacked his stomach.

"Listen, we had to. I know he doesn't like it, but I can't go about my life wondering all the time: Will he fall and break something? Will he burn up the house?"

Joseph hardly knew what to say. Tracy was exaggerating; she was overdramatizing.

"I guess he turned off the burner eventually. You should have seen all those blobs of pan metal, congealed into, like . . . weird punctuation marks."

"He was crying, Trace."

A short silence. "Look, I have to focus on the immediate problem. He's our father and he needs help."

Joseph felt for his moustache, which needed trimming again. Stray hairs of it extended over his lip and threatened to curl into his mouth. "What kind of place is it? He says he'll have to wear a uniform."

"Ha." Tracy's voice sharpened. "That's the kind of thing I mean—dementia. Do you understand now?"

He should never have said it, he saw that now.

Long after the call was over, Joseph lay flat on his bedroom rug, wishing for something, he wasn't sure what. He thought mostly of his father, the choking sound on the telephone, but occasionally his mind skipped to things Tracy had mentioned: Melissa's digestive troubles, the shortage of type O negative at the blood bank.

He had devised a bar graph depicting usage data. Blocky swaths of darkness marched across the pages until Joseph thought the eventual viewers might fall into a depression. What was this usage data anyway? The times of day, the durations, the choices, the clicks.

He would have liked to talk to someone about the jay. She had come near landing on his shoulder—flown up to it and turned back at the last minute. Three times she had taken peanuts off his leg. But Ryan had not come by the office lately; no one had.

He rummaged in his desk drawer—he was one of the few who even had such a thing. Most of the others worked at tables and had no drawers or office implements whatsoever, only laptops. One person had even said to him, "I don't do paper." And without paper, there was no need for paper clips, staplers, pencils, pens, erasers. Staple removers. It was all gone.

He found the stamp and the ink pad and set them on the desk. He stamped green images on a sheet of foolscap. Balls, balls, molecules. For the hell of it, he stamped a row of them across the bottom of his bar graph; they seemed to anchor the piece nicely. The visual.

Later, when the supervisor called him in, he had the jay on his mind once again. The blue of her wings was like nothing else in nature, except perhaps for certain flowers. Delphiniums.

The supervisor held up a page of usage data. The bar graph appeared more than ever like a town of black buildings by Le Corbusier. A finger pointed at the green images below.

"What do these represent?"

Joseph yanked his mind back from the bird kingdom. "Silicon bonded with hydrogen."

"Silicon."

"Tetravalent," said Joseph, pleased to have remembered that part of it.

The supervisor set down the sheet of paper, squaring it against the edge of the table. "Silicon Valley, is that the point?" For a moment, he seemed just a little bit intrigued. "In the future, remember to keep a lid on it."

A peanut in one hand and a glass of zinfandel in the other, he settled into his lounge chair. The tree branches swung intermittently; most of the camellia blossoms had fallen.

This time, he didn't bother setting a peanut on his leg. Instead, he held out his hand with the peanut in it and waited. He tried to calm his mind, tried to relax. He lifted his other hand and looked at the glass of zin, the rich color like *old-fashioned* draperies. He reflected that *old-fashioned* was the old-school way of saying *old school*.

The glass came to his lips; he sniffed and took a sip. Red-tasting, sweet as raisins. It occurred to him that he wanted to stay alert, hold still, and relax all at once. Wine could not be a part of that. Slowly, he lowered the glass to the concrete beside him; there was a small, grinding sound as the two hard surfaces met.

Lately, he had regretted so much; he would get this right. Instead of suppressing his breaths, he prolonged his inhalations and made the exhales even longer. He braced his left elbow against his waist so that he could hold out his hand without tiring. Sun came through the tree branches and flirted with his eyes. Now and then his hand bobbed in the air as he lost focus and then quickly caught himself.

The jay appeared without a shriek or a scramble, landing neatly on top of the wall. She barely paused before dropping to his shoulder.

Joseph held himself in an inspired paralysis. He could feel the jay hesitating, feel her tilting forward as if to jump or fly. She was still on his shoulder. He strained his eyes leftward in their sockets and saw the delphinium-blue feathers and the eye with a teardrop of light in it.

All at once she jumped to his hand, picked up the peanut, and flew over the wall. He could move now. He dropped his hand into his lap and studied his palm. She had stood there. Landed, unhurried, lifted the peanut from his skin. He still sensed the weight of her, and the grace—the way she had launched herself from his hand, the decisive flight, and her wide wings clearing the wall, off and away.

Hallie Johnston

BIRD

On Bird's eighth birthday, her mom makes a pineapple upside down cake, yellow and glazed and fruit on top. The cake sits in the refrigerator, wrapped in cellophane, and Bird can't stop thinking about wanting to steal the maraschino cherries from inside the pineapple rings. This is why she's called Bird—the way she picks and pecks at food, never in one sitting, never full bites. Also because of the way she likes to climb to the tops of trees and perch there for a while.

It would make her mom furious, Bird knows, if she were to dig out part of the garnish before the cake was even cut, so she stares out the living room window at the Magnolia in the front yard. The tree has grown taller and fuller since Bird slipped from the top four years ago, face-planting into the mud and grass. The impact knocked her two front teeth, turning them gray until they fell out.

"God-dammit," her dad says, and even though she hears it often, Bird's heart flutters. It's the word he uses when he watches college football, which is what he and Bird are doing while they wait, Bird already in her swimsuit and her dad glistening with sunscreen. Down the hall, the bathroom door opens and slams, opens and slams. Her mom and older sister, Ellis, scream at each other in bursts.

"God-dammit," her dad says again, but louder, meaner, startling Bird enough to leave the room. She moves quiet into the hall, presses her ear to the closed bathroom door. Ellis is crying, her words runny and muffled. Just as Bird makes out "I can't, I can't," the door swings open. Bird freezes before her mom, as though in stillness she could disappear. But instead of jerking Bird by the arm, yanking her closer for a spanking as she does when she catches Bird eavesdropping on the other line of the telephone, her mom goes rigid too. Her knees crack as she kneels down, holds Bird soft by both shoulders. Ellis slams the door behind her.

"Your sister," her mom begins, "she has some bleeding."

Her mom looks away, staring at the corner of the ceiling, the floor, just beyond Bird's ear. When she finally faces Bird, she twists her mouth to the side the way Bird has seen when she loses herself in thought. "Don't remember that," her mom says. "Your sister is getting older. That's all."

But she keeps talking anyway, saying certain words over and over like nature and natural, very natural and that her sister needs some time and today may not be the day she hoped. That they would save the cake for tonight and the pool for another hot afternoon. It's late August in Alabama and there would be plenty more heat.

"No," Bird says, and though she may be a year older, she can't help but stomp her foot, cross her arms as though growing younger. Her mom stands up, mirrors her pout until Bird sees her childish reflection and tries again.

"The pool closes soon," Bird says, "forever."

While her dad reads the sports section of the newspaper, Bird likes to sit at the breakfast table with him and read the community bulletin that comes in the mail each week. It has news about the town—zoning ordinances, new football coaches, when the city pools close for fall. She read where they won't reopen again until next summer, which seems like forever to Bird.

"Steve," her mom yells and then again a second later, "Steve."

Her dad walks into the hall with the TV remote still in his hand. He often does this, wanders into other parts of the house with the remote. He's always getting blamed for it going missing, found in the bathroom, the hall closet, and even once in the silverware drawer.

"Joan," he says, pointing the remote at them, eyelevel with Bird. She has the urge to swat at it like an insect. "I thought we agreed."

Bird knows about this agreement because almost every night after dinner her parents argue, yelling at each other about not yelling at each other. The fights start small—the way her dad sits on the kitchen counter while she cooks dinner, his rear so close to freshly washed vegetables, or the way her mom screws up her face whenever she talks on the telephone. She says it's her "listening face," but he says it's a "someone just died face" and why does she have to make everything seem so stressful all the time.

Then they start shouting. After shouting a while, one of them starts getting mad about the shouting, and then they shout about this. Her mother does it while cleaning the kitchen and drinking the last of her glass of wine, and her dad from the counter by the stove where he likes to loiter after dinner. The bottom cabinet keeps his gin and vermouth.

"Today is a big day for both your daughters," her mom begins even and quiet, "but it's Bird's day first. It would really be a help if you could find the time to take her out so that she has a good memory from today, maybe of something other than crying and cursing and football."

Her dad clears his throat like he's going to say something, but instead hands over the remote, landing it heavy in her mom's hand.

As Bird and her dad leave out the kitchen, her mom follows them, handing her dad his beeper he never remembers and holding open the glass door Bird once tried to walk straight through on accident. She got a knot on her forehead, but her mom still likes to Windex it transparent each morning. "Be safe," she says, making sure to hold the door by the handle, avoiding fingerprints. "Be safe, and I love you." These words have become her mom's parting ritual whenever she's separated from one of her children. It's something her dad has adopted too, and sometimes Bird is told she's loved five times a day. Sometimes it's easy for Bird to say back and sometimes, especially lately, it just feels like words.

Her mom started the "I love you" goodbyes last Christmas, right after the news about what happened to that little girl.

Even before hearing bits and pieces of the JonBenét story, Bird didn't like basements—what she knew of them anyway from playing at friends' houses. The way the sun could never really get in, the way some of them dug into the ground, too cold, too dark, especially in the corners with the wolf spiders. Sometimes, at night, Bird remembers the little girl and feels afraid but takes comfort in knowing that their house only has an upstairs and downstairs, finding solace in something she can put her finger on, something her mom can't seem to do.

As Bird and her dad drive away, her dad tries to tell the story her mom usually does—Bird's origin story. It starts with Bird coming too fast, but her mom insisting on shaving her legs and putting on mascara, almost waiting too late to leave for the hospital. This beginning part her dad gets right, but otherwise keeps missing parts and skipping parts and saying, "Well, now, let's see, maybe it was before that."

But Bird doesn't correct him, just letting him talk himself in circles because she doesn't care anyway. All she cares about now is how Ellis is bleeding and that must mean she's dying and what if when they get home her sister is dead just like that little girl.

"Take me back," Bird says and stares out her window, trying not to cry because whenever Bird cries her dad cries too. He says he can't help it, but watching her dad cry makes Bird cry harder and longer until her forehead breaks out in welts.

"I've got a surprise," her dad says. "Your favorite place."

Bird has two favorite places—outside and the dollar store. Since they're heading toward town, Bird figures it's the second, and she begins to perk up because at the dollar store everything is a dollar.

But when they arrive at the shopping center, her dad doesn't park in their usual spot but makes a wide U-turn in the expanse of the parking lot. He pulls the car up to the curb next to the store.

"Closed," Bird reads, and her dad swears again, saying he can't believe it and why does this town have to be so dead on the weekends.

"It's not dead," Bird says, thinking of Ellis not the town.

"You're right," her dad says. "We'll make our own fun."

There's a double candy machine outside the store, so her dad gives Bird eight quarters. She takes turns between the machines, cranking out handfuls of gumballs and Runts. She dumps all the candy into her pocket book, which she got last Christmas. It's clear and plastic and noisy to zip and unzip. She used to hate it, especially when she thought about the sunflower hat her sister got, similar to the one from that show Ellis always watches. Bird isn't allowed to watch the show and thinks it's boring anyway, but she likes the hat because of the flower, how it reminds her of the dandelions she plucks from the grass and tucks behind her ears. She also likes it because Ellis has one and never lets her wear it, shouting "Lice!" if Bird ever comes close to putting it on her head. Bird only had lice once in the first grade, but their mom is a woman who doesn't like taking chances, so this is all that needed to be said for her to intervene and take sides.

Thinking of Ellis now, Bird wishes she had never tried to steal her hat. That she'd only ever been as sweet as the pile of candy in her purse.

In the car, her dad rolls down the windows to let a breeze through, and they sit there for a minute, hot air on their faces, both working their jaws at a gumball. They stare out the window like there's a view, but the parking lot is as deserted as when they arrived. Feeling like the last on earth, Bird swallows hard, and by mistake, her gum too. It all sits heavy in her stomach, dissolving, if only a little, after the chirp of her dad's beeper and the message from her mom to meet at the pool in five minutes.

"Glad those two worked it out," her dad says. "I hate when they fight, don't you?

But Bird doesn't answer, just waits for him to start the car, searching her head for that word her mom calls him. *Obvious, obvious, obvious,* she thinks to herself until she finally has it: *oblivious.*

At the pool, Bird's dad chauffeurs her to the entrance where her mom and Ellis are waiting. He parks but stays in his car to listen to football. Inside the pool, Bird and Ellis follow their mom as she hunts down an empty chaise lounge. Ellis instantly dumps her stuff and joins a group of girls near concessions. Bird is made to stay with her mom until she finishes putting a bow in her hair, which she does almost every day, but always when they go swimming. It's big and bright and easy for her mom to keep an eye on, to watch bob around the pool, duck under and come back up.

"Done yet?" Bird asks, her mom still fluffing and tightening the bow.

"Can't forget," her mom says, now hitting a bottle of sunscreen against the heel of her hand. Bird hears the pop of the cap, the squeeze, the oozing of the lotion. This last sound makes Bird grin but she quickly changes face, gasping when she feels her mom's ice-cube hands. Her mom gasps too before stopping to rub her hands together, huff her breath onto each palm. But her touch is still freezing. Bird shuts her eyes to bear the pain, and when she opens them, sees the sunflower hat staring right at her, falling out of Ellis' pool bag.

"All done," her mom says.

Bird jumps to her feet, hot pavement searing her skin but only for a moment as she grabs the hat and sprints off, already having noticed the lifeguard stand and its empty chair. But her mom's call to slow down echoes from behind, forcing Bird to walk, feet and legs still moving fast, fast, fast.

She finds Ellis and a few girls at a picnic table sharing icees and cheese nachos. Most all the girls are older than Ellis by a year, maybe even with driving permits already. Bird can tell by their bikini tops and the thickness of their thighs. They talk and eat, talk and eat. Bird waves the hat like a flag, trying to deliver it to Ellis as though it were the ulti-mate apology, as though she may never get another chance.

But Ellis won't look at her. One of the girls seems to be in the middle of a story and all of a sudden the girls lean in. Birds steps closer too.

"Then," the girl says, "his mom comes up to me at the diving board and whispers, 'Honey, your string's hanging out.'"

The girls erupt in laughter, so hard they all go quiet, and Bird smiles watching them, wishing so badly she knew what was funny.

"What string?" Bird asks as the laughter begins to wane. They all turn to Bird. Ellis bugs out her eyes. "Silly string?" she asks. There's another spell of silence but the girls aren't laughing; they're staring at Bird. Then it starts again—raucous giggling—and Bird feels like the punch-line of a joke.

She throws the hat at Ellis before running toward the pool and cannonballing into the water. She wants to live here now, under water, so she stays as long as she can, surfacing only for air before plunging back down.

Bird does this for a while, submerge and emerge, as though being born over and over. When she feels herself again, she pushes off for the last time, the pads of her toes nearly raw from the rough pool floor. But this time she doesn't make it to the top, having somehow become tethered to the bottom. She feels a pinch on her big toe, like a bite or sting, but when she looks down, she sees it's the pool drain. Her toe has slipped through one of the grates, something that's happened before when she tried to fish out an earring she discovered, except this time she can't get free. With a ceiling of water above her, she wiggles her toe and turns her toe; she holds tight to her leg and yanks.

Last, she tries swimming free, arms and the one leg paddling and kicking in place until she's worn herself out just as she did earlier that summer at swim camp when she came third in the treading water contest. She became so tired she felt like she could fall asleep in the deep end, which is how she was feeling now. In the split second it occurs to Bird that sleeping might feel the same as dying, bright sunlight catches the hue of her bow. In the next moment, she's pulled hard as a rope, gasping as she breaches the surface of the water. Her mom holds her by the shoulders as she did earlier that day, but this time gripping her tight, asking her question after question but Bird has forgotten how to talk.

A lifeguard wades across the pool, and Bird feels everyone watching as she's hooked to the flotation device and pulled to the steps at the shallow end. As the pool claps, her mom takes her by the hand. The lifeguard follows them, apologizing and apologizing, saying he usually never takes concession breaks during a shift and, if he does, usually nothing happens. Bird's mom doesn't slow down or acknowledge his illogic but instead just keeps walking, holding tight to Bird until they reach the chaise lounge where she swaddles Bird in a towel. Then, finally, she turns to the lifeguard.

The last time Bird saw her mom do this, give someone a piece of her mind was when Ellis got detention the first week of school for violating dress code. That morning, Ellis went to school wearing a spaghetti strap top under a cardigan. At some point during the day, she took off the cardigan, loaning it to a friend who wrapped it around her own waist. When asked what happened to her sweater, Ellis claimed she never had one. That she came to school just as she was.

After Ellis got out of detention, she and Bird sat in the car outside the school while her mom talked to the principal. Bird could see her mom through the office window, pointing, pointing, pointing, which is what she liked to do when she gave someone a piece of her mind, which is what she's doing to the lifeguard now before he gives up and walks away. His back turned, he throws his hands in the air as though getting the last word, as though saying this woman is crazy.

Just as soon as he's left, Ellis is in her mom's face like a bee, saying to her do you know who that was? That's so and so and he does this and that and all the girls like him and did she know he's going to be a senior when she's a freshman and this is probably just about the worst thing she could ever do.

"I want to die," Ellis says. "I want to die."

Bird feels dizzy, almost sick. She's wrapped in her towel like a burrito and her eyes sting with chlorine.

"Please," Bird says, wiping her face with the corner of her towel. "Not today."

"Exactly," her mom says. "We've dealt with enough today."

She hands Ellis a towel to cover up with, and as she does, a zip-lock bag falls from its creases. Bird is first to it, nearly having it in her grasp until Ellis snatches it away, stuffing it into her pool bag and rolling her eyes.

In the parking lot, the family splits again. Her mom takes Ellis home to "rest," and Bird is told to stay with her dad. He's still in his car, and when Bird slides into the passenger seat, the leather burns the backs of her legs. She pulls them to her, wrapping her arms around her knees and hugging them close.

"Do you have dirty feet?" her dad asks, switching off the radio and the game. Everything goes quiet and Bird buries her face in her arms. "Feet off the seat," her dad says.

Bird moves one foot to the floorboard, then the other, slowly unfolding until her face is no longer hidden. She sees herself in the side mirror, cheeks splotched and red. Mistaking it for sunburn, her dad asks, "Did your mom leave the lotion?"

"I don't want to swim anymore," Bird says.

She looks away from her dad, out her window. Her dad pats her on the back but doesn't say anything until it seems the only thing he think of is to ask for a piece of gum. Bird digs in her purse, hands it to him over her shoulder, never taking her eyes off the sky where she's looking at nothing at all. It's only blue and sunshine, and the thought reminds her of the "Zip-A-Dee-Doo-Dah" song she sings to herself when she swings at recess. Usually the song makes her feel like she could catapult herself into the air and keep flying to wherever she wanted for as long as she wanted because the sky seemed endless. But when she thinks about the song now, it seems like a silly song about words that aren't words, and the sky looks like it's just a coat of paint.

But then, overhead, a familiar buzzing; the sound grows from no-where and everywhere like a giant house fly. Her dad leans out the win-dow, ducking back inside with a wide grin. He has blue in between his teeth from the gumball.

"I hear Scoot," he says, really chewing the gum. He pops it once, twice, and on the third time, starts the car, leaving the windows down as they drive away.

Once, when Bird was seven, she dared her dad to ride his bicycle with his feet. Without hesitation, he accepted, and as she rode behind him, Bird saw it all—his hands leaving the handle bars, stuck out to each side, stretching full his wingspan. And then his feet off the pedals, lifting, lift-ing, but only so far before he tumped himself off the back of the bike, skull smacking concrete.

He bled from the back of the head and onto the road, but for only a moment before he shot up to his feet, his hand pressed to the spot, winc-ing and smiling or smiling and wincing. The bleeding stopped at some point as they pedaled home, and Bird agreed she wouldn't tell her mom.

But he would end up confessing anyway, and she would call him names, swear up and down about his stupidity and immaturity as she cleaned and bandaged him. He would not need stitches; his hand had taken most of the fall. Bird remembers her mom saying over and over that the bone looked broken, to go to a doctor or else it would heal crooked. But insisting it was just a sprain, he never did.

Bird notices now the bend at the knuckle, how his finger slants just right as he stretches his hand at the top of the wheel before turning down a service road, which is the only way to get to the town airport. Scoot is the name of the man who runs it. He likes to say he owns two things in this world: a very small plane and a very large iguana. Bird heard him say this the last time she came with her dad. She also knows the iguana is named Percy. Bird doesn't know Scoot's real name, but knows he's called Scoot because of the sound he makes when he walks—shuffling his feet instead of picking them up. He and Bird's dad became friends that July after her dad turned forty and decided to take flying lessons. At the time, this was something her parents fought about for many nights and still remains a sore spot between them.

Scoot flew in the Air Force. Her dad also said he was in Vietnam and Korea and that he was a good man with a heart of gold, even a Shriner for God's sake. Her mom said that may be so but his heart was also one corn dog away from giving out, and the thought of the two of them in that tiny plane, Scoot's big belly pressed against the yoke, made her heart feel like it would give out too.

Bird first went with her dad to the airport when her mom took Ellis into the city to get her braces—there weren't any orthodontists in the small town where they lived. Before leaving, her mom made her dad promise on his life he would never let Bird go up in a plane, not with him and especially not with Scoot who was always trying to catch his breath.

That day he honored his word, making Bird stay behind in Scoot's office with Percy and a snack from the vending machine.

But not today.

Today Scoot's plane is packed to the gills—Scoot, Bird, her dad, Bird's purse. She digs around inside it for anything purple, but once the plane picks up speed, the wheels leaving the ground, Bird becomes a statue. She thinks she feels her stomach in her throat. Her dad turns around, looks at her and smiles; he puts both hands in the air like it's a rollercoaster.

At altitude, Bird swallows and swallows until her ears pop. Her dad tells her after that she could use gum for her ears but Bird doesn't understand, thinking it weird and sticky to plug her ears with chewing gum. She puts a piece in her mouth where she knows it belongs and then looks out the window at the houses that have turned to toys. Neighborhoods fade into trees and trees of woods. Her dad and Scoot have on headsets and they talk back and forth about football. Scoot pulls for Alabama, her dad Auburn, so it's not long before they talk themselves into a disagreement about the last Iron Bowl.

Then, for a while, no one talks. They just listen to the sound of the engine until Scoot tells them to look down again. The plane draws circles in the air above their own house, and Bird thinks she can see Ellis tiny on the back porch. She squints, soon realizing it's just empty patio furniture and she wonders if Ellis could be in the bathroom again or in bed sleeping, still bleeding, still dying.

The air is thin and when Bird tries to take a deep breath, she can't. She tries again, her whole body starting to run cold and hot at the same time. Her dad looks back at her, his face quickly changing from a real smile to the one he wore after falling off the bicycle. He directs Scoot to turn around, patting Bird on the knee every so often until they land.

"It was supposed to be fun" and "don't tell your mother."

This is all Bird's dad says in the moments after landing. Inside the airport lobby, the automatic doors woosh open, and Bird starts into a run, weak and noodley as she is, across the parking lot toward the surprising sight of her mom's car and the even more surprising sight of Ellis in the passenger seat.

"Get in the car," her mom says, and just as soon as she does, her mom throws the gear into reverse. Her dad tries to approach the car as she's backing out and for a moment it seems as though she might run over him.

"Where are you going?" he asks but her mom doesn't answer or come to a full stop as she shifts into drive. She rolls up the window before speeding away.

Bird can't wait any longer. Upon seeing Ellis, she feels her body become her own again, and she reaches around to the front, taking the whole passenger seat and Ellis in her arms. Her hands barely touch just below Ellis' throat, and Ellis starts making sounds like gagging and coughing and pulls Bird off her.

"Quit it," Ellis says. "Mom."

"Bird," her mom says. "Not today."

The way her mom said it wasn't mean or nice but she did snap her fingers once in Bird's direction, which told Bird she was serious, so Bird just rests her hands on the shoulders of the passenger seat, still close behind Ellis, sometimes craning her head to see if she can find where Ellis might be hurt. Ellis has her pool bag in her lap, and when she props it against the window to use as a pillow, Bird spots the zip-lock from earlier sticking out the top. In one swoop, she steals it away.

"Give it," Ellis says, almost instantly snatching it back

"Girls," her mom says, taking a quick survey of the car, her eyeballs darting this way and that then back to the road. At the next stop sign, she puts the car in park, twisting around in her seat. Bird shuts her eyes, thinking she's about to get a piece of her mom's mind, but when she opens them, her mom isn't pointing a sharp finger but instead smiling her sweetest of smiles.

"Let's all talk," she says. "Just the girls."

On the way home, Bird's mom explains to her about Ellis, about all girls, talking to her through the rear view mirror so that as Bird listens she sometimes looks at her mom and sometimes looks at herself, terrified and impressed with what she is and will become and, above all else, relieved and ready to go home.

At the house, her dad greets them at the door.

"Cake," her mom says, moving by him and into the kitchen.

"Cake," her dad says, following behind her, remote in hand.

They light the candles and sing. Bird blows them out and makes a wish she can't remember later.

Her mom hands her dad the knife, calling him Stevie and saying he's the best when it comes to slicing cake. He calls her Joanie and passes her a piece. As they eat, her mom starts the story of Bird's birth, an altogether unremarkable story aside from the shaving and mascara, but one Bird likes to hear, especially the end when her parents tell it together, her mom saying how she was born sweet and happy, how she would come into her nursery in the mornings and there would be Bird standing in her crib, arms outstretched, not making a sound for who knows how long.

From there, her dad takes over, fast forwarding a few years when Bird, still happy, still sweet, became more "full throttle" as he puts it. Bird takes this to mean adventurous, curious.

"The real Bird," Ellis interjects between bites of cake. When Ellis is finished, she spears one of the cherries from the top of the cake with her fork and places it on Bird's plate. Using her fingers, Bird tears it apart, eating one half then the next and feeling like she's just been given a lot but can't say exactly what.

After cake, the family is full and tired, but they stand in the front yard with the lightning bugs and mosquitoes to watch Bird climb a tree by twilight. She scales one of the Dogwoods instead of the Magnolia but it's tall enough that Bird expects her family will look small and distant from the top.

Suspended between branches, Bird looks down. Though she's far up, her family still looks close. Or maybe it just feels that way.

Anastasia Dreval

Candidate for Master of Sports

It happened in early fall, right before the competition. Mom called me for supper and told me I couldn't go to my shooting classes because I had to babysit my little sister Liza after school. Mom couldn't do it anymore, because she had to get back to work. I'd just started eleventh grade. On the first of September, everybody thought I'd been ill, because over the summer I lost like 10 kilos and it looked like it. I did it on purpose, because I was in love with this guy from our team, and he thought I was ugly, I guess. Nikita liked Alla. Now, Alla was the kind of person who likes to boast about *almost* getting pregnant at thirteen and insists on saying things like "expresso" when she means "espresso." I started smoking then. I didn't want my mother to lecture me, so I told her that this guy Nikita is in love with me and takes me home every day after training. He smokes Winston Blue all the time and hence the tobacco smell.

Maria Viktorovna did not really like me. Almost the entire team had long since got their rank of the Candidate, but I still hadn't. On Saturday, we took a train to Abramtsevo to get ready for the competitions. I told my mother that I would be home late in the evening and that we'd all go back together with Maria Viktorovna. During the training, I kept missing all the time, because I was angry with Nikita, who only began to talk to me after I'd lost the weight, and because this was my last competition, and I still wasn't a Candidate.

After training, Alla came up to me and asked for a cigarette. I handed her a crumpled pack of Winston's, and she suggested having a beer together near the river, and then staying overnight at her friends' country house, "What's the point of leaving today, if we have to be back in the morning?" She was also a poor shot. "Tomorrow morning we'll go to the competition together," she said. Maria Viktorovna used to say that you should know your enemy well, so I called my mother and fed her some lie about the train schedule and stayed with Alla. After the beer, we switched to some handmade cherry liqueur, which smelled strongly of alcohol. At 6:45 a.m., we left the house and went to the shooting range. My hands were shaking, and my heart was pounding.

It was foggy. The crisp morning air carried the scent of grass and gunpowder. I started warming up with some practice shots and never managed to get closer than a four on the target ring. Then, for no obvious reason, I suddenly sensed that I would start to hit the target better. Despite the mess with Nikita, who finally started talking with me. Despite my mother saying I couldn't train anymore because of my sister, who's not old enough to take care of herself. Despite lying to her and drinking all night. Despite all of this, it seemed to me I'd hit the ten, just like in a movie. Soon enough, the warming up session was over, and my result was the worst of the group.

The competition began. I took aim. Fired. A ten, right in the center. I took aim again. An eight. And then a ten again. It all ended very quickly, I ran to the results table and shouted, "I'm a candidate!" Nikita awkwardly patted me on the shoulder.

Maria Viktorovna grudgingly said, "Finally. You could have done better, though."

But I didn't care. I was a Candidate for Master of Sports at last.

I haven't trained since then. My sister Liza started first grade, and I would pick her up from school after I finished my classes at university and take her to music school. I knew that Alla never became a Candidate and gave up shooting. I told my mother that I broke up with the guy who used to take me home, and that now I smoke myself. The next year, I was expelled, and I had no idea what to do next.

Today, I received an invitation to join the military. I think they invited everybody who had gotten their candidate rank in shooting. I imagined the army. Probably, it would also smell like gunpowder, fresh morning air and autumn grass, and I would shoot again. I took the rest of the mail out of the post box and went back to the flat. The decision didn't have to be made immediately, but my hands were shaking, and my heart was pounding.

In the next room, my sister began her piano practice. I imagined her growing up without me and threw the invitation away.

Halina Duraj

Moheem

The Wallistons—friends of friends of Kat—had an old carriage house on their estate that they lent to artists for a month in the summer. The only conditions were respect for the grounds and willingness to be trotted out by the hosts at a weekly dinner. Kat preferred her houseplants to most humans, but could ape a livelier version of herself, what she imagined non-poets expected of poets, one night a week in exchange for a carriage house—just a shack, really, Alice Walliston, had said on the phone. Kat had heard it was no shack.

It was slow at the Albany Airport taxi stand: a line of twelve yellow mini-vans and no passengers waiting, other than Kat. "Need a cab, sweetie?" a plump, pink-faced man with a wide white mustache asked Kat from the seat of the first cab in the line. She did not want to get in a cab with a man who called her sweetie. She kept walking and stopped at the minivan directly behind his. The passenger window was down. She leaned over to greet the driver, and he looked up from his phone, surprised. He had a thick salt-and-pepper mustache and wore a gray wool cap pulled low toward his brows, though it was a sunny day.

"320 Corbin Road? Exit 28?" Kat said.

He got out quickly and came around to take her suitcases. Smiling, he said, "Corbin Road, Corbin Road." Then he shook his head. "I do not know it." She put his accent in the vague general category of Middle Eastern.

"Exit 28?" she repeated, as if this time he might know it.

"On 97?" he asked.

"I don't know, sorry," she said, shrugging.

"Okay, Okay," he said. He heaved her suitcases into the back of the minivan. She slid open the side door, but he gestured to the front seat. "Please, sit up front."

"Oh," she said, "Okay." She did not move.

The pink-faced mustache man eased himself out of the first cab and asked Kat's driver, "Where you going?"

"Exit 28!" he called, slamming the rear door of the minivan. "Please, have seat," he said to Kat. She was still standing on the sidewalk by the front passenger door. She climbed in.

"Just like to know where my drivers are heading, sweetie!" The plump man called out to her, his palms out as if to ward off accusation. She rolled up her window as the driver swerved into the flow of airport traffic.

At the first stoplight, the driver offered his hand across the console and told her his name. Moheem. She gave one quick business-like squeeze—was it weird that a cab driver was shaking her hand? Any weirder than a cab driver insisting she sit up front? She didn't know. She didn't want to be rude. She felt bad for cab drivers—Uber drivers stealing their business and all.

She said her own name, then repeated his as a question—"Moheem?"—to make sure she was pronouncing it correctly. "That's beautiful," she said and wondered if a man might blanche at the compliment. She had meant it was a beautiful word—she loved words, their flavors and music; she collected them. Moheem: she'd remember it.

She pulled her hand back but he would not let go. He said his name again, as if he were correcting her, but it sounded to her exactly as she'd said it. Dutifully, though a little annoyed, she repeated it. He smiled and shook his head slightly. This time he spelled it before saying it, holding her hand the whole time. "M-o-h-e-e-m. Moheem."

"Okay," she said. "Moheem." She felt a little panicky, her hand captive in a stranger's for so long. She pulled again; still he did not let go. She jerked her hand back, forcefully, and this time he did let go. God, she hoped he wasn't a creep. She'd woken up at 4:45 a.m. in L.A. and she was tired and hungry and cranky. She couldn't deal with a creep.

But Moheem didn't seem like a creep. He asked her questions. How was her flight, why was she here—work or tourism? Had she been here before? She told him she was here for work but did not elaborate. She knew that spending days thinking about words, building poems, didn't seem like work to most people. It hadn't to her parents.

Moheem was talkative but soft-spoken in a way that seemed almost shy. He had bad breath—not food breath, like onions or garlic, but real bad breath, rotting-gums kind of breath. The cab's air felt muggy and musty, too, but Kat did not want to roll down the windows. She did not want him to think that she found the climate or smell in the cab disagreeable. She took off her blazer and folded it in her lap.

Moheem asked her where she was from.

"Originally? San Francisco," she said. Although he looked over, his eyes didn't quite meet hers, as if he were looking at something outside her window; she wondered if someone was passing on the right.

"I have visited San Francisco. Golden Gate Bridge, Fisherman's Wharf, Mountain View," Moheem said.

"Oh! I grew up near Mountain View." She did not name the town she really grew up in, the affluent Peninsula suburb of Atherton, where her Polish parents had made a down payment on a house long before she was born, after a decade of frugal living in a studio apartment in the Sunset. A construction worker and a cleaning lady could do that that back then, in the sixties, in the Silicon Valley—save to buy a house in a quiet, pretty neighborhood.

She found herself wanting to tell Moheem that she was the daughter of immigrants—only a generation removed from him and whatever his struggles were. But that generation was a chasm, she knew. She couldn't presume to know anything about his struggles. Her English was native; she taught it, for God's sake. Other than her last name—Wilkowski—betraying her Polish-ness, she spoke, acted, carried herself like an American, whatever that was. Her first name had been shortened for her by her kindergarten teacher—from the formal Katarzyna, a Polish version of Katherine. She hadn't really cared—she probably would have changed it herself soon anyway. Her parents had never called her Katarzyna, only Kasia, its tender diminutive.

"Where are you from?" she asked Moheem.

"Pakistan," he said. She nodded. She had picked up an anthology of contemporary Muslim-American poets at Skylight recently, but she could not name any Pakistani ones. She knew of Iqbal, no one else.

"I like California very much," Moheem said. "Very nice, very pretty. Clean, very safe."

"Well, I don't know about safe. It's not always safe," Kat said, thinking of the pepper spray she usually carried in her purse, except for when she flew. Moheem did not say anything.

"Although, I guess compared to much of the rest of the world, it is very safe," Kat said.

"Yes," he said, nodding. She got the sense she'd narrowly avoided a certain kind of ignorance.

"How many years have you been in the U.S.?" Kat asked.

"Oh, a long time," he said. This time his eyes met hers. "Half my life there, half my life here."

She nodded. He was wearing a gray fleece zippered jacket with a Governor Cab logo. The sleeves were too short and his wrists stuck out, hairy and bony. They seemed delicate, small, almost feminine, other than the thick, dark hair. She noticed his fingers—long and narrow, elegant, with a sprinkling of dark hairs on the knuckles. She wondered if he'd been a brain surgeon or concert pianist before he left Pakistan—one of those brilliant, accomplished people toiling invisibly in America for the sake of children back home or born here. She thought of her father's hands, scratched and scarred. Moheem caught her looking at his hands, and she looked out the window.

When she looked forward again, Moheem glanced over and she followed his gaze, pitched low again. Did she have a stain on her shirt? She looked down. Of course, she had something on—or rather, under—her shirt. She pulled the soft fabric of her long-sleeved tee-shirt away from her breasts. It wasn't a tight top, but the fabric clung.

"What do you like to do for fun in Los Angeles?" Moheem asked, definitely looking at her breasts. She crossed her arms over her chest.

"Go to the beach, hike," she said, staring straight ahead.

"Oh, you like to hike?"

She wanted to say, "Yes, my breasts like to hike, asshole." She just nodded.

"You like to drink, smoke?"

"Excuse me?"

"Drink alcohol?"

She recrossed her arms. She pursed her lips and pretended to think about it, as a way of stalling. She didn't know how not to answer without seeming stuck-up.

"No, not really. Occasionally. A glass or two of wine a week."

"Scotch? You like scotch, whiskey?"

"No, not really," she lied. She did: a finger of Macallan 12, neat.

She did not ask him if he drank alcohol. She hunched forward, elbows on knees hip-width apart, like a skier. She let her shoulders round so that her breasts in their bra-cups hung into the loosened tent of her tee-shirt, the fabric falling away. Her left arm shielded the curve of her left breast. She thought about putting her blazer back on and just feeling hot, but somehow that seemed worse than this contortion.

They drove in silence for a while, and she looked out her window, craning her neck as if not to miss a single tree.

"Very beautiful around here," Moheem finally said. "You go to Lake Placid while you are here. I give you my number, show you around."

"Oh," she said. "Thank you." She wondered if he was offering to drive her around in the cab, with the meter on, or if he meant it like a date. "I think I'll be pretty busy working while I'm here. Thanks anyway."

Then she added, "You know, my boyfriend loves New York. He's from Buffalo."

The topic of a boyfriend revived Moheem's questions: what did her boyfriend do? How long had they been together? How old was he? Older, younger? Moheem was fifty-four, he told her. Was she happy with him, her boyfriend? She made up answers to all of these questions, since she did not have a boyfriend. Yes, she was very happy with him. She began asking her own questions, he couldn't ask her any. When in the fall did the colors start to change? How long would they last? When did the first snow usually come? Was this weather typical for July?

Then Moheem asked her whether she had pets. No, he asked her breasts whether they had pets. She looked at the meter: Fifty bucks already.

"No," she said, "my breasts don't have pets. Do yours?" She rolled down her window and took deep gulps of air rushing past her face, blowing her hair back. If he responded, she didn't hear it. They drove for what felt like a long time.

She felt relief when she saw a sign for Exit 28 and he took it. The exit turned into a tee at a frontage road. A sign indicated "Old Corbin Road." "Right, left?" Moheem murmured. Kat could have sworn Alice had said there would be a stoplight right off the exit. Kat rummaged in her bag for the Post-it note with her scribbled directions but could not find it. She had taken the Post-it with the address and gate code, and there it was, partially stuck to mini-pack of facial tissue, but where was the folded up sheet with the directions? Was she panicking and therefore passing her hand right over it? She did that sometimes.

Out of politeness, Kat had taken the directions Alice Walliston insisted on giving her over the phone. She began them on the Post-it note, under the gate code, but when she realized how long they'd be, she grabbed a sheet of paper out of her printer. Kat had been puzzled. She had the address; weren't cab drivers supposed to know their way around? "Just in case," Alice had said. "Our place can be a little complicated to find."

"Which way?" Moheem asked. Cars pulled up behind them. One honked, then another.

"Sorry, sorry!" she said, still rummaging. "I don't know. Maybe left?" She pulled out her phone and entered the address: 320 Corbin Road. The creeping blue dot revealed they were going in the wrong direction. The red pin indicated the Wallistons' estate was back up the highway, the direction they'd come from.

"I think we were supposed to take a right back there," Kat said. She looked at Moheem's phone stuck to the dashboard with a little arm: the phone's screen was dark. "I thought you'd have GPS in the van," she said, trying not to sound too accusatory. There was no point in asking him to turn it on now—she was already using her phone.

"I thought I did not need it, because you knew where you are going!" he said.

"I never said I knew where I was going. What made you think that?"

She heard how they sounded—a bickering old married couple lost on vacation—and it would have been funny if she were not becoming slightly frightened at being lost and alone in a vehicle with an agitated man she didn't really know and no pepper spray.

Moheem made a U-turn on the frontage road when there was a break in the cars, but as they neared the exit, the phone instructed them to get back on the highway, in the direction of the airport. "I guess? Try it?" she said to Moheem when he looked at her—her eyes this time, not her breasts.

They got on the highway, and at the next exit, the phone told them to get off, get back on, and go in the other direction, Exit 28 again. "What? Oh good Christ," she said. "Yes, yes, fine. Get off. Go in the other direction. Take Exit 28 again." Moheem did as she said. Could she be stuck forever in this endless loop, in an airless cab with a breast-ogler, the meter ticking upward? Sixty-five dollars now. Would she have to pay the whole price for this indignity? Why was she looking up the directions on her phone and telling him where to go?

She knew why. Because now that she was repeating the directions right from her phone, she liked the feeling of being in charge. "Get in the right lane. Okay, turn here."

The red pin signifying the Wallistons' house on the screen seemed eternally to the left of the blue dot representing them, this infernal cab. They seemed to be driving just past the house, and yet she couldn't even see a driveway from the road.

Kat instructed Moheem to turn around, make a U-turn. The third time she said it—it *had* to be here—he threw up his hands.

"No, it is not here. I try something else." Instead of turning around he kept driving, sped up, in fact, and she saw the red dot receding now as they moved further down the road. Ahead was a thickness of trees—that dense, overbearing New England tangle, choking the road from the sides and overhead.

"It's not this way," she said. "Turn this car around. Right this minute." She knew she sounded imperious but she was scared enough not to care, finally. Moheem muttered in another language. In spite of her burgeoning fear, she felt a prick of shame that she had no idea which language was spoken in Pakistan.

He took a hard left, and they careened at high speed along an even more deserted road along a creek—the kind of creek, Kat thought, FBI agents fished dead women's bodies out of. If they didn't see a house or a car by the time she counted to ten, she would call the police. She counted to ten, then over again.

"Turn around," she said, her voice now squeaky and thin. "Go back." She couldn't believe this was happening, how the story of her life would end.

"I'm looking for your house!" he yelled.

"Turn around right now," she said. She felt her body's urge to piss out of plain fear—something she hadn't felt since she'd been a little girl. "I'm calling the police if you don't." She looked wildly around the cab— wasn't there a sticker somewhere, with the cab's I.D. number? They could track her phone, they would find her. She remembered the pink-faced man. He could tell the police where to begin the search.

"No, no police. Not necessary to call the police!" He made another left turn, too fast, and she got thrown forward and against the door, jerked against the seat belt when it caught.

"Let me out," she yelled. "Stop this car, let me out." She touched her fingertip to her phone screen: the nine, then the one.

"No," he said. "No need. Please, please. We are almost there. What is the house number?" His "please" had an edge of desperation to it, and the desperation scared her more than captivity—desperate people do desperate things, she thought. Don't provoke.

"The house number," he said again. "See, I am looking for the house. See? Please!"

He had slowed down, and they were passing imposing gates, long shaded driveways. Was this Corbin Road? She fished the Post-it from the top of her purse; it quivered in her hand. "320," she said, trying to keep her voice even, calm, matching his. She kept her finger poised over the green "dial" button on her screen.

He was slowing now and, then speeding up, looking frequently in the rearview mirror. He peered out the driver side window. "You look that way," he said, and she did. There were no houses visible from this road either, but they were passing stone pillars marking long shaded driveways that disappeared into their own tunnels of trees.

Finally, Kat saw the stone pillar with "320" in brass and the wrought-iron gates Alice Walliston had mentioned in the shape of two massive steel swans, necks tucked, beaks touching. A local blacksmith had forged them for her, she had told Kat. Look for the swans! You can't miss them, she'd said.

"See, no police, no police," Moheem said, shaking his head. He was smiling, as if to reassure her, but his eyes had fear and maybe a little remonstrance in them. She bristled. She'd been the one awash in fear. Why was he—ah. Of course. A visa, maybe.

The property was colossal. They crossed a bridge over a small pond partially shrouded in weeping willows. Then the minivan trundled toward a three-story stone manor with gables and turrets and a porte-cochere over an imposing front entrance. There was a tower at the far end of the house—no, not a house: a small Bavarian-style castle. Sloped lawns extended all around to more trees, other small, elegant buildings. One of them was probably the carriage house, she realized. They passed another small pond in which a pair of real swans—white—idled.

Moheem pulled under the porte-cochere and parked. Even though it was only late afternoon, the interior of the cab was dim enough that Kat couldn't read the bills in her wallet. Moheem turned on the dome light. One more awkward interaction, Kat thought. She looked at the meter.

She shouldn't have to pay eighty dollars for this drive. The quote she'd seen on the Internet said fifty; a different woman—one who would have said, "Hey, buddy, my eyes are up here," or "I don't feel comfortable answering that"—that woman would negotiate. But she was not that woman. She was the woman who wanted to get out of this cab, fast. She handed him her credit card.

"Oh," he said, with slight dismay. "You pay with card?"

"Yes."

"How much cash do you have in there?" he asked, nodding toward her wallet.

"Excuse me?"

"Cash. How much cash do you have?"

No cab driver had ever asked her such a question, no person she'd ever done any kind of transaction with, actually.

"But I want to pay with a card," she said. She knew she didn't have enough cash to cover this, though she could do a cash tip. And why was he asking?

"But how much cash, how much?"

The front door opened and the butler emerged. Alice Walliston had told her they hired one for their weekly dinner parties; he wasn't there the rest of the week, she had said, as if apologizing for her little indulgence. And then it was all happening at once—Moheem asking her again how much money was in her wallet, the butler opening the passenger door, Alice Walliston coming down the front steps, short silver bob, bleach-tray smile, a cream and gold brocade-trimmed jacket, tailored black trousers.

"I'd rather not say," Kat said, in the haughty tone she used when she was most deeply ashamed. Moheem pulled a face, the expression her mother had made when Kat had been obstinate as a little girl.

"I'm using my card," Kat said, "and that's it." She thrust the card toward him.

Moheem took it, ran it through the card-reader. She fumbled in her wallet. Not a good tip—he hadn't done his job! He'd ogled her breasts! He'd practically abducted her. A five was too little. But twenty percent on the meter? That wasn't right either. She decided ten was a fine-though-not-great tip on what the fare should have been, had they not gotten lost.

Silently, Moheem handed her the doubled slip. She signed and handed it back to him with the ten folded underneath.

"Thank you," he said, without looking at her.

"Thank you," she replied, then hated herself a little. What was she thanking him for? But still: her mother had taught her you thanked people who worked for you, no matter what.

The butler extended his hand to help her step from the minivan onto the diamond-patterned pavers. "Welcome, madam," he said. She waved his hand away. "Oh, thank you, no, I'm fine," she said. Moheem pulled out her two battered suitcases with the pink yarn ties at the handles. She reached for them.

"Allow me, madam," the butler said, hoisting the suitcases and lifting them away from his sides as he walked, Kat noticed, as if they might contaminate his uniform.

"Have a very nice stay," Moheem said. Then: he looked in her eyes. "God bless you," he said.

It was a real look, not an ogle, and tinged with pity. She could see that he thought she needed it, God's tenderness or mercy or something. She felt as if she was supposed to say something in return—thank you, or God bless you, too, but she did not want to thank him for his pity and she did not believe in God. She felt too angry, too stiff to say anything. Also, she did not understand why she felt so sorry, so sad, as if some terrible misunderstanding had taken place. What had gone wrong? Where?

Kat let Alice sweep her toward the door, enfold her into her welcoming chatter—You must be so tired! How was the flight? Direct? Still, I know how it is! How about a cup of tea? Something stronger? A martini? Oh, the restroom? Of course, it'll be at the end of the hall. Dinner at seven, just a few neighbors. We so want to hear about what you're working on! Do you like Cornish hen?

Kat glanced over her shoulder in time to see Moheem's minivan cross the bridge and disappear among the willows.

After dinner, Kat inspected maps of the area on her laptop. She saw evidence of what Moheem had suspected and Alice had explained over crème brulee: there was another Corbin Road parallel to the frontage road but even further in from the highway. That inner road was simply Corbin Road—no Old—and the frontage road was Old Corbin Road. "Oh my god," Kat had said. "Why didn't they just give the new road another name?"

Alice shrugged: something about local tradition, the county road-naming committee, and the Daughters of the American Revolution. Corbin—"Captain Molly"—was an unlikely war hero; she took over firing her husband's cannon at the British when he died in the Battle of 1776.

Before dinner, Alice had given her the tour of the carriage house, pointed out the deck with the hot tub and the fully stocked wet bar and showed her, of course, her studio, with the big oak desk under a window and the laminated card with the wi-fi access code—but only if she wanted it! Kat thought about looking up the cab company and filing a complaint. She hadn't told Alice about the strange ride—she didn't entirely understand what had happened herself, and telling the story too soon would be like pinning down something still alive, fluttering with possibility.

It was near midnight. She inspected the bed and found the kind of down-topped mattress she'd once melted into at a ritzy hotel. The sheets were starched Egyptian cotton, she suspected, with a thread-count higher than her monthly salary. But she was nowhere near sleep. She inspected the wet bar, poured herself a finger of a Scotch she'd never heard of, tasted it, swooned slightly—a different plane than Macallan—and took the tumbler to the desk under the window.

She opened her laptop. She didn't bother to pull the thick damask drapes. She could see the glowing windows of the castle across the lawn, oddly comforting. She wondered where the swans slept at night. Wings folded, on the pond? Did they tuck in to a mudbank somewhere? She opened a browser window and typed "how swans sleep."

At dinner one engine of her mind had figured out why Moheem asked her about the cash in her wallet. But all the other engines were trying to solve that look—that glimmer of tenderness, or pity.

She'd have to write a poem about it: it was the only way she ever figured anything out. She typed "Moheem" at the top of a Word document.

She didn't know what to write next, so she switched back to the browser and searched "languages spoken in Pakistan."

She counted the Wikipedia entry's list. Not one language. Sixty-four, at least. There were national languages and provincial languages and sub-provincial languages. There were major languages and minor languages, official languages, unofficial languages, co-official languages. There were colonial languages and immigrant languages and literary languages. There were regional languages and regional sub-provincial languages. And all of them had beautiful, beautiful names.

Her thoughts tumbled like scree. She had bypassed the first taxi, the man who'd called her "sweetie," and chosen Moheem instead. She had just done it—instinct. She'd been tired, she didn't know taxi stand rules, didn't know you didn't choose your taxi out of the line-up like cuts of meat at the butcher's. You got in the first cab in the line. But she hadn't. Moheem didn't know why, didn't know he was just the first inoffensive driver in the line. He must have interpreted her rejection of the first taxi driver as an intentional selection. She'd sent him a message. And then she'd told him he had a beautiful name.

She took a sip of Scotch and opened a new browser tab, typed "Governor Cab Albany," and called the number. As it rang, she took another sip of Scotch. And another.

"Governor Cab." The dispatcher's voice was female, tired, and curt. Kat tried to sound brisk and confident.

"I'd like to speak to an employee, he's a cab driver. Or maybe a manager. I don't know his name—he's kind of, he had a white mustache, kind of heavy-set guy? I saw him at the airport today. He seemed to be in charge. Of the other drivers. How could I speak to him? When is he usually in?"

There was a long pause. "Melvin? You want Melvin?"

"Maybe," Kat said. "I mean, no. I don't want Melvin. But I'd like to speak to Melvin, maybe. If it's the same person. Does he have a mustache, kind of pink—complexion?"

"Hold on, let me see if he's here."

Her heart beat more quickly, her throat clamped. She made a practice noise, and her voice came out a croak.

She heard distant voices through the receiver—a low female one, a gruff male one, then both coming closer. A rustling, a receiver being picked up. A male voice: "This is Melvin, how can I help ya?"

"My name is Kat Wilkowski," she said. Her voice was a little wavery but not croaky. "I'm calling because—were you working at the taxi stand at the airport today? This afternoon? First cab in the line, around 3:30 p.m.?"

"Might have been. You leave something in a cab?"

"No. Yes. Sort of. Please don't call women 'sweetie.' I'm not your sweetie. Thank you." She hesitated. "God bless you," she added. She hung up. Her heart thudded.

She went into the bathroom, looked in the mirror, and practiced. *Don't call me that, put these bags in the trunk, shut up and get me where the hell I want to go.*

She laughed. She liked how she sounded—brash and forceful, a little old-fashioned, like a character in an old movie. She said it over and over. She had so much fun saying it that when she finally felt sleepy and climbed into bed, she thought she might hear it in her dreams. But that night she dreamed only in languages she didn't yet speak.

Bonnie Omer Johnson

Book Review: *Victorine* (Fleur-de-Lis Press, 2020)

by Drēma Drudge

Drēma Drudge's debut novel *Victorine* opens with an eighteen-year-old Victorine Meurent, no longer modeling for an unappreciative painter—Couture—but teaching guitar lessons in her father's shop, where he creates and produces advertising posters and signs. When Edouard Manet enters the shop, seeking Victorine as *his* model, he promptly hires Victorine, despite the fact that she now has a broken nose, thanks to her boyfriend. She becomes Manet's model for his most famous and most scandalous paintings—*The Picnic on the Grass* and *Olympia*—but Victorine also moves in and out of studios and meetings with many other now-famous painters.

In many ways Victorine is a thoroughly modern woman, ambitious and self-aware: "My boldness comes upon me in dashes, in flashes, as I realize those around me have not lived what they meant to. I will not, cannot do the same. . . . I must find a life that fits, and I have not." She wants to be not only an inspiring model but also a recognized painter herself.

Walking alongside her into seamy places, the reading audience celebrates Victorine's eventual success as an artist when her work is accepted into the prestigious Paris Salon, where her self-portrait will hang in the gallery reserved for Manet and other worthy artists whose last name begins with the same letter—Room M—now also for Meurent.

Neither the novel nor the character pander for audience approval. Rather, the novel is its own large canvas of rich bold colors and shadows, with light and dark tones, bringing alive this woman with an intense passion for both life fully lived and art fully realized. From childhood, Victorine desires to guide her own ship: when her teacher suggests that her young student might like to study porcelain at a school for women, Victorine exits—mooning her teacher before she goes out the door.

Life as well as art is the subject of Drudge's novel. The narrative of *Victorine* includes war, loss, death of Victorine's father, her husband, and of Manet; Drudge paints for us many of the Parisian places inhabited by artists—cafes, taverns, apartments, grand homes, galleries—as we pass the likes of Rodin, Degas, Morisot, and Monet.

The character Victorine delves into relationships and fragile egos, leaving us with truths that cross centuries: "Idealizing people on canvas is another way of saying you love them, that they are even better than they imagine."

By the final pages of *Victorine*, readers understand and appreciate her as an influence on the Paris art scene of the day. Drudge successfully brings Victorine forward to take her rightful place among the French artists, where the female artist offers up the sum of her journey: "I'm in Room M, the place I've been looking for, it seems, since I was born. I have created myself. I will be seen."

To call this a coming-of-age novel is an injustice. I find it easier to talk about what Victorine is not as to define what it is. It is not a morality tale, a travelogue, a history, or a depiction of Parisian society prior to the Victorian age. Yet, it is all of that. And More. With a capital M.

Not only will Victorine be seen—Drudge's intention for writing the book—but also the author herself creates a place to be seen in the literary world with this, her very own, work of art.

Mary Popham

Book Review: *A Tale of Three Women* (Excalibur Press, 2021) by Kathleen Thompson

In *A Tale of Three Women*, Kathleen Thompson has created an authentic, down-to-earth novella, but one imbued with magical elements. Although her characters are fictional, the Alabama town of Brownville has a real antecedent, built in 1927 by one of Louisville's millionaires, J. Graham Brown. He and his brother owned many businesses, and the small village was created for the purpose of housing the workers in their wood-preserving business.

Thompson's haunting description, with remarkable attention to detail fueled by informed imagination, brings the recent past of rural Tuscaloosa, Alabama, roaring to life again. We are transported to the streets and pause to observe the buildings: across from the commissary where food and supplies are charged to private accounts and are deducted up front from one's payroll check, a company doctor sees his patients. Next door is the small post office whose postmistress holds letters until someone comes in to inquire, as does Mydearie Mae one day: "Do you have *my* letter?" The community center serves double duty—a place for worship and entertainment.

The author remembers the town well, as her family lived in one of the small homes made of black wood—the same creosoted product of black tar chemicals that protects telephone poles and railroad ties from the sun, rain, termites, and fungi.

The theme of love circulates around and through the events in *A Tale of Three Women*—not only romantic and familial love but also love of place. Indeed, the setting has the presence equivalent to that of another notable character. The main road is paved, others are dirt; some houses have closets and a large claw-footed bathtub; windows are open during summer, and a coal heater often stands in the middle of the main room. Smells in the town vary from the rotten egg aroma of the creosote to the sweet steam from a boiling pot of greens. Happy sounds fill their simple lives: while the factory whistle begins their day, it also signals that the shift is over; on TV, Rowdy Yates and Opie reign; and the Baptists and Methodists alternate their Sunday services.

Thompson's story focuses on three women, two of whom have nothing in common but their names. However, the name is *not* common: Madeira Mae Smith. The reader easily keeps them apart, as one is spelled differently: Mydearie Mae. The third woman is Betsy Slowe, a librarian, and a former schoolmate of the latter. All three women love the same man—James C. Slowe, a talented wood-carver, whose whittling could have made him a great artist but for happenstance's twist of fate. His four-blade Fighting Rooster knife, which he sharpens every morning, has carved mostly animals—squirrels and birds—from cedar. But his prized piece was a mahogany pterodactyl. It could never be duplicated. "'Ain't no two alike,' he said. 'If I whittle now till doomsday, I couldn't get that same wing lift or that big, pointy beak.'"

As fictive years pass, Thompson examines the lives of the three woman and the different manner of love from each one for Jimmy Clyde, as James Slowe is also known. The circumstances in Jimmy C.'s life bring him the pain of separation from his small town. He suffers severely, sometimes doubling over, crying. "Homesick is one thing, but when you know you can't ever go home again, now that will nearly claw the bottom of your gut open."

And what had the older Miss Madeira Mae promised him? There is a mystery in Brownville, folded beyond the memory of most residents. It would be criminal to divulge the secret . . . rather, the reader may gather clues and suspicions and see how it stacks up in the end. "The story takes hold of you," remarked the author's close friend, Helen Norris, a former Alabama Poet Laureate. Truly, this delightful novella ranges from train tracks, to college aspirations, to the famous Alabama Lane Cake. *A Tale of Three Women* offers much about life to contemplate, both past and present. As modern readers follow the timeline, from past to present, the extensive changes made since this older era are likely to be uplifting.

Cornerstone

work by writers K-12

Nanditha Nagavishnu

SLEEP IN A MOVER'S PARCEL

i lost this city dreaming in the bed of a chambermaid
or so it looked like, for when i opened my eyes

she was balancing a taper candle on her head
and her body was waxed in the gelatinous seal

the thin lined: this is my room, all in this corridor and then some.
it was with luxury of guest-ship that i plumed this self
on being able to only swallow, as thinking out loud is doing it.

in a week, the flimsy curtains dusted like a dynasty
and the existential pool of waking suns shushed to droplets,

the chambermaid still had a face that glowed like she
herself swallowed the light, in all her bulging-in-the-middle
skinless cupidity, her hair mussed with the tiniest

sculptor chipped strands grazing the camphor flicker
near her candle, now a crinkling lost-bride searchlight,

though she balanced it on her head like the
ladies their terracotta water pots on turbans,
as silk wrapped an hourglass body like turbans,

big waxy dowry of a thawing height,
small dowry of a thawing feeling, why does bland

wax drip down a skin in cocoons, is he pale now?
when i opened my eyes, uh, room twisting, chambermaid

melting from her toes, dripping on the bed-legged ceiling.
i am losing this city dreaming in a cardboard room,

ancestors' tongue clicking at my doll arms, and every other
blink losing me a banana tree, a vendor with a billhook

neck, arms stained tender coconut green. courtyard home
with a girl cleaning around the cardamom, tugging
on braids that almost choke the wick-thin ladies.

Nicole Chu

How Inopportune

I never asked for a portent,
never called on any divine facility.

But here you are,
alive and altogether
"put."

In retrospect,
I suppose that I was,
in some measure,
aided by what you bore.
But I,
nevertheless,
would have appreciated some restraint,
on your part.

In truth, I rather like to think
that I am in command of my own form.

So I would understand if,
in the event that you are unlawfully contradicted,
you disappeared.
Because, quite frankly,
I had not missed you.

Nicole Chu

A Series of Assessments

Tonight, the sky is a glaring coal,
a truly pallid swathe.

I can state that it is still,
but transient,
and just shy of a limb.

However, as I now grasp it,
I cannot comprehend the flexibility
with which it treats my hand.
It seems to have been drawn anew.

I would like to revise my analysis.

I can state that it is limp,
tired,
and altogether faraway.

Nicole Chu

Optimism

Those persistent, frank tablets of Sun;
Observe how hard they work to counteract the rain.

Evelyn Coen

WRITING IS LIKE

A birth
With every character,
You are born all over again
And get another try at life

A sunset
A waterfall of colors
A cascade of ideas
Falling into
A cup
Slowly filling until
It overflows
And the ideas bubble up

They're never still,
They change and move,
Take shape and color,
Lines and grooves
All around you.

Spoken words aren't enough,
But written words get through.

Agnes Loeser

Rainy Meadows

Squish, squish
Slosh, slosh
The ground sinking under my rain boots.
Squish, squish
Slosh, slosh
The rain keeps on pouring.
Squish, squish
Slosh, slosh
The fields covered with the flooding rain of love.

Jaiden Galecki

KING T-REX

Stomp, stomp the T-rex goes,
On the soft soil he prints his toes,

He roars aloud for all to hear,
 To tremble and run away in fear,

T-Rex, oh T-Rex, your teeth are sharp,
To eat your prey and tear them apart,

You're tall and big from side to side,
Your tail so long they'll leave in flight,

Eep, Eep, Eep is the call,
To run away from your fierce jaw,

Your strength so mighty who can stand,
You'll fight everyone in your land.

Lily Egol

GROWING PAINS

body   c r e a k s
    like six screen doors.

give me ice cream
& i'll shove it in my face.

i want

   a boy

to like me.

i hate mirrors.

look at me: a
gangly

s
k
y
s
c
r
a
p
e
r ,

     a portable circus,
a bellowing accordion:

s t r e t c h i n g   a n d   g r o a n i n g—

goodbye, favorite shorts
hello b-cup bra.

    rice krispie knees
    go snap-crackle-pop

                                        bedhead 24/7
          & i'll probably have braces for
                                   the rest of my
                                              life.

                                        why
                                  are
                          my
                     legs
                longer
           than
my   entire torso?

i am
                                                                      a
hail-
                                                                 storm
of
                                                            hormones.

3 servings of kale slaw
2 zits on my forehead
1 lonely girl
                                        d i s s o l v i n g
                                              in
                                                t
                                                e
                                              a
                                                 r
                                                  s

Lily Egol

INFATUATION

it isn't fair

why can't I finish my breakfast
without pausing to wonder whether you
like pancakes or waffles and
pour in your milk or cereal first

how do I spend hours
drumming idly on my armchair, remembering
the way the wind whisks up your bangs

your name invades the corners
of each of five math worksheets; it
tiptoes through raindrop constellations on my window,
susurrates beneath the steady song of the radiator,
creeps into morse code tapped by my restless toes

oh look, there's your shadow sitting on my staircase;
you've moved into my house

and you don't even know

Lily Egol

SOLILOQUY

listen.
mom is in the kitchen finishing her taxes
me, i'm still here, thinking
sprawled on the rug and gazing at the ceiling
outside the world barrels forward, tainted
with pollutants and prejudices, things i didn't see until
this year when my eyes were forced open

middle school:
rumors creeping their way through the hallways
have to relearn english and watch your tongue
or you sound like a freak. too much slang,
too many rules: don't wear long skirts or you look like a grandma
and don't eat too much or you look like a pig
and don't ask too many questions for god's sake it's weird
not to mention the classes
the books you read and the videos they show you
at night i lie awake for hours, remembering

just throw all this weight on us
they've decided it's us who have to figure it out
because they haven't figured it out themselves
someday they'll all die
and we'll inherit the world

i'm still here, trembling

squeeze my eyes shut and wish
i could scrape off this year. return, return
to the child curled up inside
back to the time i didn't know what sex was
or that the oceans are slowly being poisoned. remember
when school meant picture books and crafts and
make-believe on the playground, remember

the world is slipping away and i'm still here, crying

tried to tell mom about the snickers in class
the lies and the betrayals and the eyes in the hallway
and the teacher who snorts at us, cursing our phones
so this is what's become of the next generation
the next generation doesn't know what we are

i couldn't find the words
and besides she wasn't listening

my best friend left me
ran away during lunch with the others
they thought it was funny to abandon me,
blinking in confusion and wondering
how i'll ever get used to it
if this is just middle school
how will i survive when i'm older
if i can barely survive just this

but life hurtles on
and i'm still here, trying

Lily Egol

Teenage Paradox

you say Be Yourself
but who myself is changes every day

you say Grow Up, Don't Be A Baby
but you yell the house down if i stay out too late

you say Stand Up For What You Believe In
but when i defend a stranger it becomes Mind Your Own Business

i say
give me time
there is so much i don't yet know

Ajay Sawant

HAMLET

Maggie does her dishes splendid by the
croc board
to break them seventh time running for propane over Hamlet
Like every time—there's no exhaust in the window
so it's mostly wide open
Like the last and the preceding time—the smoke escapes through
    the large opening

"What a waste of five dollar bill" her mind cries
"she burnt the book"
"she burnt the book"
"she burnt the book"
after praise and eight she had still quite not understand it
"My Taco chime is excessively fiery," says

who let fire make another remnant on wooden flooring

The grill creeks and the squires outside sizzle
with pork
why buy a book for the glory of cover
Why she irons bones under eyes for
mother's praise

From the wellspring that borders the house, a flood or drought
The salt line within corners pleading to protect spirits or
    mutinous demons
Five yards apart she floats wanting to breathe
her heart—a ocean weed deep submerged within

Ajay Sawant

ON LOVING: IN FORESTS OF OREGON

Oregon, nineteen
twenty years back

poison—green thickened, a forest consumed us
tenderloin hands rustled, then triggered
impatience slithering to shape goosebumps

just the instinct of want—
would hammer the bombshell

a spokesman hanged—
an open mouth

Oregon, thirty-nine
this sundown to night

in this fall, the tropic is old and dying
the throat parched, it cannot swallow
 but lay—asleep

dusk to dust, the pond is now a reservoir—
an open new lake of youth

just as the last leaves—
would leave masses perpetually without promises

a thickened darkness in bluets
        —a light sheen
in a rundown on integrity

NOTES ON CONTRIBUTORS

JULIE BEALS was formerly an editor at the Smithsonian Institution, but is now schooling to be a speech-language pathologist. She hopes to work in adult rehabilitation with people who have brain injuries. She has one desk for her speech affairs; another for her fiction writing. Her stories have appeared in *The Broken City* and *The Write Launch*.

D. A. BECHER is a retired attorney and current staff writer for Montana Senior News who lives in Charleston, West Virginia, during the academic year but summers in Montana. His work has garnered awards from West Virginia Writers, Inc. in the Emerging Writers, Mystery and Romance categories. His writing has been accepted for publication by such diverse periodicals as *Suspense Magazine*, *WestWard Quarterly*, *Floyd County Moonshine*, *Trillium*, *Scarlet Leaf*, *CUA Magazine* and *Edify Fiction*.

CARL BOON is the author of the full-length collection *Places & Names: Poems* (The Nasiona Press, 2019). His writing has appeared in many journals and magazines, including *Prairie Schooner*, *Posit*, and *The Maine Review*. He received his PhD in Twentieth-Century American Literature from Ohio University in 2007, and currently lives in Izmir, Turkey, where he teaches courses in American culture and literature at Dokuz Eylül University.

CHRISTOPHER BUCKLEY'S recent books are *Agnostic* (Lynx House Press, 2019) and *The Pre-Eternity of the World* (Stephen F. Austin State Univ. Press, 2021). He has recently edited: *The Long Embrace: Contemporary Poets on the Long Poems of Philip Levine* (Lynx House Press, 2020); and *Naming the Lost: The Fresno Poets—Interviews & Essays* (Stephen F. Austin State Univ. Press, 2021).

K. J. BUNDY earned a Master of Liberal Arts and Science at Vanderbilt University, with a capstone project centered around Eudora Welty's "June Recital." She is currently working on a novel about the feral children of the 1970s. One of her short stories was published this summer in the literary magazine, *Halfway Down the Stairs*.

ROGER CAMP lives in Seal Beach, CA, where he tends his orchids, walks the pier, plays blues piano and spends afternoons with his pal, Harry, over drinks at Nick's on 2nd. When he's not at home, he's traveling in the Old World. His work has appeared in *Rust + Moth*, *Midwest Quarterly*, *Gulf Coast*, *Southern Poetry Review* and *Nimrod*.

PETER COOLEY was born and educated in the Midwest and has lived over half of his life in New Orleans, where he was Director of Creative writing at Tulane University and is now Professor Emeritus. He received the Marble Faun Award in Poetry and an Atlas Grant from the state of Louisiana. Father of three grown children, he published his eleventh book *The One Certain Thing* (Carnegie Mellon University Press, 2021) this year. Cooley is Poetry Editor of *Christianity and Literature*.

TODD DAVIS is the author of seven full-length collections of poetry, most recently *Native Species, Winterkill,* and *In the Kingdom of the Ditch,* all published by Michigan State University Press. His writing has won the Midwest Book Award, the Gwendolyn Brooks Poetry Prize, the Chautauqua Editors Prize, the Bloomsburg University Book Prize, and the Foreword INDIES Book of the Year Silver and Bronze Awards. He teaches environmental studies, creative writing, and American literature at Pennsylvania State University's Altoona College.

ANASTASIA DREVAL is a Russian emerging author of short fiction. She graduated from Moscow State University and Sorbonne (Paris 3). In 2020, her Christmas short story was published in *Pashnya,* an online literary magazine. In 2021, she won the Creative Writing School short story contest, so she is to attend a course of creative writing in the spring. When not writing, she works as production manager in Masterskaya Brusnikina Theatre. Anastasia's Russian to English translation of her short story "Candidate for Master of Sports" was reviewed by Ulyana Egof and Sean Stewart.

SONAM DUNGTSO graduated from Bard College with a Master's Degree in Environmental Science and Policy. She is a translator of Tibetan, Chinese, and English. She lives in Chengdu, China, and is very passionate about education and youth development.

HALINA DURAJ's stories have appeared in *The Harvard Review, The Sun,* and The 2014 *PEN/O. Henry Prize Stories* anthology. Her debut story collection, *The Family Cannon,* was published by Augury Books and was a finalist for a Council of Literary Magazines and Presses' debut fiction award. She teaches at the University of San Diego.

LYNN GORDON'S fiction has appeared in *The Southampton Review, Ruminate, Epiphany, Baltimore Review, Zone 3,* and other magazines. Lynn lives in Northern California.

LILY GREENBERG is a poet from Nashville, Tennessee, and a third-year poetry student in the University of New Hampshire's MFA Writing program. She works as a research writer for her university and serves as Editor-in-Chief of *Barnstorm Journal.* Her poetry has appeared in *storySouth, Third Coast Magazine, River Heron Review* and she is the recipient of the 2020 Dick Shea Memorial Prize in Poetry. Twitter: lily_greenberg Instagram: lilygreenberg

KATHLEEN GREGG is a graduate of the Author Academy program through Carnegie Center in Lexington, Kentucky, during which time she was mentored by Jeff Worley, the 2019-2020 Poet Laureate of Kentucky. She is active in the Kentucky State Poetry Society, presently serving as treasurer. Her first chapbook, *Underground River of Want,* will be published this year by Finishing Line Press. Kathleen lives with her husband and one cat on five acres just outside of Lexington.

SAMINA HADI-TABASSUM is a professor at Erikson Institute where she teaches courses in cognitive and language development. She has published poetry in many journals including *Tin House, Copper Nickel, Clockhouse* and *Mosaic*. Her first book of poems, *Muslim Melancholia* (2017), was published by Red Mountain Press. She recently published short stories in the *New Orleans Review, Chicago Quarterly Review* and *Another Chicago Magazine*.

ELIZABETH HUGHEY is the author of *Sunday Houses the Sunday House* (University of Iowa Press), *Guest Host* (National Poetry Review Press), and *White Bull* (forthcoming from Sarabande Books). She is a co-founder of the Desert Island Supply Co. (DISCO), a literary arts center in Birmingham, where she teaches poetry in the public schools.

MARCIA L. HURLOW'S first full-length collection of poetry, *Anomie,* won the Edges Prize. She also has five chapbooks. More than 400 of her individual poems have appeared in literary magazines, including *Poetry, Chicago Review, River Styx, Nimrod, Poetry Northwest, Stand, Cold Mountain, Zone 3*, and *The Journal,* among others. In 2019, she received the Al Smith Fellowship for Poetry for the second time. She is the co-editor of *Kansas City Voices.*

KEN HOLLAND has had work widely published in such journals as *Rattle, Southwest Review,* and *The Cortland Review.* Recent/forthcoming in *Chariton Review, American Journal of Poetry, Confrontation*, and *San Pedro River Review.* Three Pushcart nominations, several contest wins, and work included in a number of anthologies.

EMILY JENNINGS is a writer and medical coder living in Berea, Kentucky. Her work has been featured in *Uppagus* and the *Scarlet Leaf Review.*

BONNIE OMER JOHNSON received an MFA from Spalding University and began teaching at Bellarmine U. in 2006. She, with author Kimberly Crum, conceived and curated *The Boom Project: Voices of a Generation,* published by Butler Books in 2019. When their book-marketing schedule came to a standstill with Covid-19, Johnson and Crum started an online literary publication called *Landslide Lit(erary)* on medium.com and recently started a YouTube Channel (BoomProjectBook) where they conduct interviews with authors for authors who read and talk about the writing life. Bonnie Johnson also owns The Write Place where she meets with private students seeking guidance for their writing projects and will again offer writing workshops beginning mid-summer at 4850 Brownsboro Center, Louisville. For more information, see the website: bonnieomerjohnson.com or email her at bonnieomer.johnson@gmail.com.

HALLIE JOHNSTON lives in Alabama where she teaches English at the University of Montevallo. She holds an MFA in creative writing (fiction) from the University of Miami. Her fiction has appeared in the *Southern Humanities Review* and *Sinking City.*

BRANDON KRIEG'S most recent poetry collection is *Magnifier,* winner of the 2019 Colorado Prize for Poetry chosen by Kazim Ali. He teaches at Kutztown University and lives in Kutztown, PA.

PETER LEIGHT has previously published poems in *Paris Review, AGNI, FIELD, Beloit Poetry Review, Raritan, Matter,* and other magazines.

GABRIELLE LEJEUNE is an emerging writer, born and raised in Ohio, attended Case Western Reserve University, and currently lives and works in New York.

ROBIN LIPPINCOTT is the author of six books, most recently *Blue Territory: A Meditation on the Life and Art of Joan Mitchell.* His fiction and nonfiction have appeared in over 30 journals, including *The Paris Review, American Short Fiction, Fence, Provincetown Arts,* and *The New York Times Book Review.* The recipient of multiple Yaddo fellowships, as well as a fellowship to the MacDowell Colony, he has been on the faculty of Spalding University's brief-residency Master of Fine Arts in Writing Program since 2001. He lives in the Boston area.

ELMO LUM's short stories have appeared in *Narrative, New England Review, StoryQuarterly, Conjunctions,* and elsewhere. To get by he continues regular work in San Francisco, but he has completed a novel and is working on additional projects.

SOFIA MACHADO is a current adult student majoring in "something" with the intention of doing "I don't know." An unpublished poet, she spends much of her time writing while simultaneously attempting to keep up with her energetic Border Collie. She has impressive collections of teacups, rocks, and journals that she's afraid to write in.

MELISSA MADENSKI has taught and written throughout the Pacific NW at the Northwest Writing Institute, and in public and independent schools, jails, libraries and community colleges. Her poems and essays have been published in anthologies and magazines. Her first chapbook of poems, *Endurance,* was published by Finishing Line Press in 2015.

SHERYL MASSARO is an oil painter, poet, and photographer based in historic Frederick, MD, where she is a resident artist at The Griffin Art Center. Massaro holds an MFA in Creative Writing/Poetry from The American University and studied with several key poets, including Allen Ginsberg, Stanley Kunitz, W.S. Merwin, and Galway Kinnell. She has had residencies at Yaddo (New York) and St. Peter's (Canada) colonies. She has begun a new collection of poems on the many aspects of water.

JOHN DAVID MORGAN is an Army Veteran, and thanks to the G.I. Bill, a first-generation college graduate with degrees from Bellarmine College in Louisville and Vanderbilt University. While he works in the insurance industry, he is quickly approaching a much-anticipated retirement. His first published story was in the April 2020 edition of *High Shelf.* His story "Uncle Polly and the Three Megans" was selected as a finalist, and included in *The Saturday Evening Post 2021 Great American Fiction Contest Anthology.* John's daughter suffers from depression, and his son is a heroin addict.

Keith Morris earned his BA from The University of Mississippi and earned his MA from Mississippi State University. He teaches English at Itawamba Community College in Fulton, MS. His poems appear in *FishFood, Sonder Midwest,* and *Cathexis Northwest Press.* His latest music can be found at https://keithmorris11.bandcamp.com/releases. He lives in Tupelo, MS, with his wife and two sons.

David O'Connell's work has appeared in *The Cincinnati Review, New Ohio Review, Copper Nickel, Sugar House,* and *North American Review,* among other journals. O'Connell's first full-length collection, *Our Best Defense,* is forthcoming from Červená Barva Press in 2021.

Dr. Emily Jane O'Dell is an Associate Professor at Sichuan University-Pittsburgh Institute in the People's Republic of China. Previously, she held the Whittlesey Chair of History and Archaeology at the American University of Beirut and was an Assistant Professor at Sultan Qaboos University in the Sultanate of Oman. Stateside, she has taught at Columbia, Brown, and Harvard, where she did her Postdoctoral Fellowship, and she has also been a Research Scholar in Law and an Islamic Law and Civilization Research Fellow at Yale Law School and an editor for Harvard Law School's *SHARIASource.* Her research can be read in the *Journal of Global Slavery, Journal of Iranian Studies, Journal of Africana Religions, Obsidian: Literature & Arts in the African Diaspora, International Journal of Persian Literature, Journal of Literary and Cultural Disability Studies, Disability & Society,* and *SHARIASource* at Harvard Law School. Her writing has appeared in *The New York Times, Al Jazeera, NPR, CounterPunch, Salon, The Christian Science Monitor,* and *Huffington Post.* She received her MFA in Literary Arts at Brown University.

Derek N. Otsuji is the author of *The Kitchen of Small Hours,* winner of the 2021 Crab Orchard Review Poetry Series Open Competition. It will be published by SIU Press in fall 2021. His poems have appeared or are forthcoming in *The Threepenny Review, The Southern Review, Rattle, Poet Lore,* and *Pleiades.*

D Larissa Peters just moved to the West Coast after living in Baltimore, MD for over 10 years—in the middle of a pandemic! Baltimore was only one of the many cities she has lived in the last 40 years. She has a BA in English, which she uses as much as possible in her job at the relief and development organization she works for. She appreciates a good conversation that lingers over the right kind of Kentucky bourbon, and it was Louisville where she discovered one of her favorites.

Mary Popham is a 2003 graduate of the Spalding MFA in Writing Program. Her novels set in Central Kentucky in the early 1900s are *Back Home in Landing Run, The Wife Takes a Farmer,* and *Emmalene of Landing Run.* She has also published a collection of short stories, *Love is a Fireplace.*

Lisa Rhoades is the author of *The Long Grass* (Saint Julian Press, 2020) and *Strange Gravity* (Bright Hill Press, 2004). Individual poems have appeared at *Barrow Street, Poetry*

East, Prime Number, Saranac Review, South Carolina Review, and *SweetLit,* among others. In addition to teaching poetry, she works as a pediatric nurse in Manhattan. Lisa lives on Staten Island with her spouse and their two children. Find her online at: amazon.com/author/lisarhoades and http://lisarhoades.com.

A line volunteer at the Northern Indiana Center for Hospice Care and the Beacon Children's Hospital Ronald McDonald House, **DAVID RICCHIUTE** is the author of two poetry collections, *Uncertain in the Worst Way* (Main Street Rag Publishing, 2020) and *So Everyone Else Will Know* (Aldrich Press, 2018). His research appears in the *Journal of Applied Psychology* and *Journal of Experimental Psychology* and his fiction & poetry in *NOON, POEM, The American Journal of Poetry,* and *Tampa Review,* among others.

KRISTEN ROACH is obsessed with Mata Hari, spinning fire, and the radioactive wolves of Chernobyl. She lives and writes in an old tavern on the College Highway in Connecticut. In the past, her poetry has been hosted by *Gravel, Sugar House Review,* and *pif Magazine.* Otherwise it roams the streets.

CAROL SCHAECHTERLE has published poetry in *Pebble, Mad River Review* and *Midwest Review.* Wearing her academic hat as Carol S. Loranger she has published studies of the poetry of E.A. Robinson, Paul Laurence Dunbar, Robert Frost and, most recently, Sanora Babb. Her edition of *Told in the Seed and Selected Poems of Sanora Babb,* is planned for release in late 2021.

JOAN SELIGER SIDNEY is Writer-in-Residence at the University of Connecticut's Center for Judaic Studies and Contemporary Jewish Life. She's the author of *The Way the Past Comes Back* (The Kutenai Press), *Body of Diminishing Motion: Poems and a Memoir* (CavanKerry Press), *Bereft and Blessed* (Antrim), plus many poems in literary journals and anthologies. *Body of Diminishing Motion* won an Eric Hoffer Legacy Finalist Award.

WILL SIMESCU grew up in Northern Michigan and spent six years as a Russian language analyst in the U.S. Air Force. He currently lives in Fort Collins, Colorado, where he studies Restoration Ecology at Colorado State University. He was a finalist for the *Ember Chasm Review* 2020 Summer Poetry Contest and a semi-finalist for the *Nimrod International Journal's* 2020 Francine Ringold Awards for New Writers. Simescu's poems have also appeared in *Slippery Elm* and *Plainsongs.*

ALEX SHULL is 45 years old and has lived in Louisville, Kentucky, most of his life. He has two children. He is a software developer and lifelong poet. Shull's poem, "Your name on me," was written last year.

TARUNI TANGIRALA is a student who resides in the Houston area. She serves as the founder and editor-in-chief of *Réapparition Journal,* an online journal for poetry and prose that addresses chronic illness, and her work has been named a semifinalist in the national

Women on Writing contest. In her free time, she enjoys watching movies such as *Inception* and *The Imitation Game*.

TARA TULSHYAN is a high school sophomore currently living in Manila. Her works have appeared in *K'in* literary journal and Rising Phoenix Press, among several others. She is currently working on a collection of poems that are inspired by her home, the Philippines.

LUKE WALLIN's recent poetry and cover art have appeared in *The Louisville Review, Canary,* and *Sisyphus.* He holds an MFA from Iowa and has written books on conservation writing as well as novels for children and young adults. He taught at The School of Visual Arts in Manhattan, The University of Massachusetts Dartmouth, University College Dublin, and Spalding's MFA in Writing program.

M J WERTHMAN WHITE is an Ohio poet. She is a past recipient of the Paul Laurence Dunbar Poetry Prize and The Antioch Writers' Workshop's Judson Jerome Poetry Prize and Scholarship. Her first book of poetry, *How the Universe Says Yes to Me* was published by Main Street Rag Press in 2017.

NOTES ON CONTRIBUTORS TO CORNERSTONE

NICOLE CHU is a ninth-grade student living in southern California. She is a member of her school's Mock Trial team and French Club. Nicole has, since 2012, greatly enjoyed the practice of creative writing and poetry composition. After she graduates, she plans to major in English and ultimately pursue a career in writing. In her spare time, she enjoys learning new songs on the piano, creating decoupage projects, and collecting Precious Moments figurines.

EVELYN COEN is an eleven-year-old middle schooler who loves to read and write. Her dream is to become a famous author and win the Newbery Medal. She has lived in Columbus, Ohio, all of her life.

LILY EGOL, a high school junior from New Jersey, has been writing since she was four years old. She has participated in the Columbia Advanced Creative Writing Workshop as well as the Advanced Track Creative Writing program at Interlochen Center for the Arts. Lily has also received silver keys from the Scholastic Art and Writing Awards, been published in *Cricket* magazine three times, and been awarded runner-up in a playwriting contest sponsored by the Royal Shakespeare Company. She is interested in poetry, playwriting, and fiction. This collection, "Growing Pains," is written in the voice of her middle school self and explores the turbulent experience of growing up, both physically and emotionally.

Jaiden Galecki is a 12 years old middle schooler who lives in Southwest Florida. This is the first poem he ever made, and he is happy to share it with you!

Agnes Loeser is a 6th grade honors student at St. Francis of Assisi School in Louisville, Kentucky. Her favorite subjects are biochemistry and literature. In her spare time, she enjoys competitive gymnastics, listening to music and making art.

Nanditha Nagavishnu is a sophomore at Coppell High School in Texas. Apart from creative writing, she contributes as a writer to her school newspaper, *The Sidekick*. She loves reading anything confessional. *The Louisville Review* is her first publication.

Ajay Sawant currently serves as Editorial Chief at Globalage Poetry and Editorial Intern at *Five South* magazine. He is a student from Pune of Maharashtra, India, simultaneously pursuing BA Hons. in English. He is an art activist and public speaker. His recent poems appear in *Detester Magazine, Vayavya,* America's *Art & Understanding Magazine* and forthcoming in *Xavier Review*, The Virgin Island's *The Caribbean Writer* and *Hawai'i Pacific Review.* Ajay can be reached on Twitter @ajaycycles.

About the Back Cover Artist

Laurie Fader has shown widely in the United States and Europe and participated in residencies that include the American Academy in Rome, Scuola Grafica di Venezia, The International School of Drawing, Painting and Sculpture in Umbria, Italy, the Alfred & Trafford Klotz Residency in France, and a Painting fellowship in Haiti. She has been honored with a Pollock-Krasner Grant and Adolf and Esther Gottlieb Foundation award, a Helen Winternitz Award for excellence in painting from Yale, a Founders Day award from NYU and others. Fader received an MFA from the Yale School of Art and a BS in painting from New York University Tisch School of the Arts.

Fader's early practice focused on contrasts of industry and residential neighborhoods in Brooklyn, NY. After 9/11, she moved to Baltimore where she created large landscape paintings that were sparsely populated with figures or animals, suggesting a story that was at once intimate and universal.

Fables, or cautionary tales, with narrative elements embedded in labyrinthian corridors of color, shape and form can be found in her recent work. A feminine heroine is often central to her abstract landscapes.

Fader has held teaching positions at the Yale School of Art, Pratt Institute, MICA, Goucher College and was the Director of The Kentucky College of Art and Design at Spalding University in Louisville, Kentucky, where she currently resides as a full-time practicing artist. Fader's paintings can be viewed and purchased at her website, lauriefader.com.

www.ingramcontent.com/pod-product-compliance
Lightning Source LLC
Chambersburg PA
CBHW030742110726
47900CB00008B/2417